You Can Write for Magazines

GREG DAUGHERTY

WRITER'S DIGEST BOOKS
CINCINNATI, OHIO

Other fine Writer's Digest Books are available from your local bookstore or direct from the publisher.

Visit our Web site at www.writersdigest.com for information on more resources for writers.

To receive a free weekly E-mail newsletter delivering tips and updates about writing and about Writer's Digest products, send an E-mail with "Subscribe Newsletter" in the body of the message to newsletter-request@writersdigest.com or register directly at our Web site at www.writersdigest.com.

07   06   05   04   6   5   4   3

Library of Congress Cataloging-in-Publication Data

Daugherty, Greg
   You can write for magazines / Greg Daugherty.—1st ed.
     p.   cm.
   Includes index.
   ISBN 0-89879-902-3 (pbk. : alk. paper)
   1. Freelance journalism. 2. Authorship. 3. Feature writing. 4. Technical writing.
   I. Title.
PN4784.F76 D38   1999
808'.02—dc21   98-48930
                                                             CIP

Edited by David Borcherding
Production coordinated by Erin Boggs
Production edited by Jeff Crump
Designed by Pam Koenig
Cover design by Mary Barnes Clark

ABOUT THE AUTHOR

Greg Daugherty has been both a magazine editor and a freelance
writer for more than twenty years. As an editor he has held senior
positions at such magazines as *Money, Consumer Reports, Success*
and *Reader's Digest*. As a writer, he has contributed to many
magazines and major newspapers, authored one previous book and
coauthored another, written a twice-a-month on-line column and
served as a *Writer's Digest* correspondent since 1987. Currently
he is editor in chief of *New Choices: Living Even Better After 50*
magazine, part of the Reader's Digest Special Interest Magazine
Group.

TABLE OF CONTENTS

IF I COULD, YOU *CAN*

For the past twenty years I have been lucky enough to make my living as a magazine editor and writer. I have assigned and edited articles for seven different magazines at last count. And I have written for so many others that I have totally lost count.

So I guess I qualify as something of an insider in the magazine business now. But I can still remember what it was like to be an outsider, someone who yearned to write for magazines but knew no one in the field except the kid down the street who sold subscriptions door to door. Naive as I was, I believed that editors were gods, that New York was the cradle of civilization and that if I could just get my proverbial foot in the proverbial door. . . .

What did I do? I bought a book, much like this one, and read it until I could have recited it from memory. With that book's advice and encouragement, I studied magazines like a real writer, sent out my first queries, collected my share of rejections, and gradually proved to myself and others that I could write for magazines.

During the past two decades, I've learned that some of my early notions about magazines were way off the mark. I now know that editors are not gods (though a few of them may think so) and that New York is not the cradle of civilization (that was ancient Mesopotamia). But I also know that if you can just get your proverbial foot in the proverbial door, you'll have a terrific time.

On the pages that follow, I'll share with you the most useful things I've learned during my years inside the magazine business. I'm glad I had that book I mentioned earlier to guide me along. But I really wish that twenty years ago I'd had this one.

1 HOW MAGAZINES WORK, AND WHERE FREELANCE WRITERS FIT IN

Legend has it that the term *free lance* made its first appearance in Sir Walter Scott's novel *Ivanhoe*. Scott used it to characterize soldiers of the Middle Ages who weren't committed to a particular king but instead offered their lances in the service of any cause that struck their fancy.

Freelancing may no longer be such a dashing occupation, but then again, today's freelancers don't have to worry about being hit over the head with a truncheon. Most of the time, anyhow.

Freelance writing has its own noble tradition. For as long as there have been magazines, editors have relied on freelance writers to supply the words. Men and women as diverse as Albert Einstein, Eleanor Roosevelt, Harry Houdini and Woody Allen have freelanced for magazines.

Today, demand for freelance magazine writers—particularly good ones—is strong. The reason is economics. Magazines are becoming more and more specialized. As a result, they have smaller circulations and can't afford to maintain large editorial staffs. To keep their pages filled with fresh and lively material, they must turn to freelancers.

That's the good part. The rest of the story is that freelancing has always been a tough way to make a living and probably always will be. It is not a get-rich-quick proposition; it's rarely even a get-rich-slow one. But as much as writers like to complain about the difficulty of their labors, I've been struck by one simple fact in working with dozens of them over the years: I have never met a freelance writer who wanted to do anything else.

Whether freelancing is a full-time occupation or a part-time pre-occupation, you'll benefit from a knowledge of the inner workings of magazines. Not surprisingly, many of today's most successful freelancers apprenticed on magazine staffs earlier in their careers. While no two magazines may operate exactly alike, the step-by-step process that will be outlined here and explored in greater detail later in this book is pretty representative.

STEP 1: THE ASSIGNMENT

Freelance writers win their assignments in a couple of ways. Often they'll approach an editor with a story idea in the form of a query letter. Other times the process is reversed, and a magazine editor will approach a writer with an idea.

Obviously, the better known a freelancer is, the more likely that an editor will call. How do you become "known"? One tactic is to gradually establish yourself as an expert in a certain subject area, such as sports, health or money management. When an editor needs a piece on that topic, it's your phone that will ring first.

Article assignments are usually confirmed by letter, sometimes by a formal contract with all the appropriate legalese. Among the terms an assignment letter or contract will cover are:

- The length of the article, usually measured in words.
- The deadline or due date.
- The rights the magazine wants to buy. For example, first North American serial rights.
- Payment.
- "Kill fee." This peculiar invention of the publishing business refers to a token sum that will be paid if the writer completes the article, but the publisher decides for one reason or another not to use it. Usually a kill fee is 20 to 50 percent of the agreed-upon payment.

Some assignment contracts go into far greater detail than this, but these are the basics. (For more about contracts and other business matters, see chapters seventeen and eighteen.) And one more thing, which veteran freelancers know but many novices do not: The terms of an assignment contract frequently are negotiable.

What about manuscripts that arrive at magazine offices unassigned? Many of them go right back into the self-addressed, stamped envelopes their authors have courteously enclosed. With the exceptions of fiction and poetry, magazine writing is generally a collaboration between writer and editor from the idea stage onward. Writers whose nonfiction manuscripts show up uninvited seldom have much hope of publication, except at the smallest of magazines.

Obviously, this can be a discouraging situation to writers trying to break into magazines. It's a lot like getting your first job: You can't get a job unless you have experience and you can't get experience unless you have. . . . You know the routine.

One strategy for beginning writers is to offer to take an assignment "on spec." This means the magazine won't owe you anything, even a measly kill fee, if the article you do proves unsuitable. Writing on spec is a risky proposition and not something you'd want to do for the rest of your career, but it's sometimes a way to break in.

STEP 2: WRITER AT WORK

If a magazine needs an article for its next issue—because, say, the news is hot, or the editor just forgot to assign it earlier—the writer may have to deliver a manuscript within a matter of days following the assignment. Or, if the subject is unusually complex or requires a good deal of travel on the writer's part, the magazine may set a deadline months into the future. Under most circumstances, though, monthly magazines give writers about four weeks to complete an assignment.

As long as we're on the subject of deadlines, one last etymology lesson. Know where the word *deadline* comes from? From a line drawn around military prisons beyond which wandering prisoners would be shot. Writers who don't take their deadlines seriously would do well to take heed.

During the reporting and writing period, writers may hear again from their editor or they may not. Editors differ vastly in their habits. Some of the more obsessive types will call daily to see how the article is going. Others may send along an occasional newspaper clipping or note of encouragement. Still others will simply hang back and let the writer go about his or her work.

In any case, when questions come up during the course of a writer's research that could affect the article, most editors are grateful to hear from the writer. Often a writer will have discovered a more interesting angle to the story. Other times, the basic hypothesis of an article will, after some digging on the writer's part, turn out to be false. On those occasions, an editor is particularly glad to find out what's happening before a finished manuscript appears in the inbox.

Meanwhile, behind the scenes at the magazine: While the writer is hunched over a keyboard, the editor probably isn't giving that particular article much thought. Not that the editor doesn't care how it turns out. The reality is that magazines work on several issues at a time, each at a different stage of production. In early October, for example, an editor may be reading the final proofs of the November issue, editing manuscripts and approving layouts for the December and January issues, and making assignments for February and beyond. An article that isn't even in the pipeline yet tends to not get a lot of attention.

STEP 3: THE MANUSCRIPT ARRIVES

It's deadline day, and there in the editor's morning mail is the freelance writer's manuscript.

It better be. Nothing so aggravates an editor as a manuscript that for whatever reason doesn't show up at the appointed hour.

Editors, of course, aren't always so punctual. On the day the manuscript arrives, the editor may be leaving for a two-week vacation. Or the manuscript may just sit in the editor's inbox for days, as he or she attends to other matters. Whoever first noted that life isn't fair was probably a freelance writer.

But let's suppose your article has arrived on (or, bless you, *before*) your deadline, and the editor has immediately torn open the envelope to give it a read. What happens next? One of several things, depending on the magazine.

If the article looks fine to your editor on first reading, it may be photocopied and circulated to other editors on the magazine's staff for their comments. If it appears to need more work, the editor might call with suggestions for a rewrite. If the article strikes the

5

editor as beyond repair, the editor may decide to reject it, entitling you to the dreaded kill fee.

Let's say that the editor is basically satisfied with the manuscript but thinks you need to strengthen some parts of it. You'll probably get a good-news/bad-news phone call. The good news is that your article is right on target, a delight, a pleasure in every respect. The bad news is that it's just the slightest bit weak on pages 1, 2, 3, 4, 6, 9, 12, 14 and 15. The editor is sending it back to you for further work.

Beginning writers are sometimes bruised by an experience like this. Veteran freelancers expect certain articles to require a second run through the word processor, and they build time into their schedules to accommodate one.

Along with a request to do more work will come a new deadline, usually just a few days or a week away. You may already have the information the editor wants somewhere in your notes; otherwise, it's time for some crash research.

Meanwhile, behind the scenes at the magazine: Even if the completed manuscript isn't in hand yet, the editor now has a pretty good idea of how to package your article for publication. He or she has been talking to the magazine's art director about the layout and about any artwork or photographs that need to be assigned.

Somewhere deep in the editor's subconscious, a headline for your article is coming into focus. As most long-time freelancers know, it's generally a waste of effort for writers to put headlines on their own articles. An editor will change it anyway—to something worse if necessary. Spend your time on the article instead.

STEP 4: ACCEPTANCE!

OK, the rewrite of your article has been accepted. Congratulations. Now you're free to go on to your next project, right? Sorry, not yet. Depending on the magazine, writers are often involved in the production of their articles right up to publication and sometimes even after.

During the period immediately after your article is accepted, copies will go to the magazine's fact checkers. Not all magazines have fact checkers, but the larger, better ones do, and from a writer's point of view, they can be quite annoying. Fact checkers will want backup for every factual statement in your article, particularly ones that could leave the magazine open to a charge of libel. They may ask you to send copies of clippings, interview notes and whatever else you used in your article; they may spend a lot of time on the phone with you, verifying that someone's scarf was indeed teal and not aquamarine. Fact checkers may seem bothersome, but their role is to make certain that neither the magazine nor its writers embarrass themselves any more than is customary. Be kind to them.

Then there are copyeditors. The editor who assigned your piece will do a preliminary edit on your manuscript, concentrating on the big picture: structure, content, tone and so on. After that, the manuscript will usually go to a copyeditor, who focuses on such details as spelling, grammar and style.

Style, in the magazine sense, means a set of rules about how a publication handles punctuation, abbreviations and other nitpicky stuff for the sake of consistency from article to article. Many magazines have their own internal style manuals. Others use the style manuals available in bookstores and libraries.

Copyeditors often view themselves as the English language's last line of defense against illiterate barbarians (in other words, the rest of us). Though that does at times cast them in an adversarial role toward writers, a conscientious copyeditor is really the best friend a writer can have (excluding, of course, the person in the accounting department who writes the checks).

Meanwhile, behind the scenes at the magazine: Aside from the fact checker and copyeditor, other magazine staffers will be helping ready your article for publication. The art department will, in collaboration with your editor, have decided how it will look on the page. A photographer or illustrator may be at work as well.

STEP 5: ALMOST THERE . . .

Your article is due out in just a couple of weeks. You've squared matters with the fact checker and the copyeditor. Maybe you've received your check from the magazine. Maybe you've spent it.

Some magazines will send you galley proofs of your article at this stage, so you can see it in type and, they hope, catch any remaining errors. Others leave that to their staff editors.

7

If this seems like a quiet time to you, it's the busiest time of all at the magazine. Here we go again:

Meanwhile, behind the scenes at the magazine: Your article is six lines too short for the layout. An editor (maybe the assigning editor, maybe the copyeditor, maybe the brand-new editorial intern) will have to insert enough words here and there to add six lines.

Or else it's nine lines too long. The same cast of characters will have to do some judicious trimming.

Or it's fifty-four lines too long. (Don't even *think* about what's going to happen.)

That's sometimes the reason words you don't remember writing appear in the finished version of your article. Or a paragraph you labored over for hours disappears.

Also, the photographs or illustrations will have arrived by now and been placed in the layout. An editor will write captions for the photos, tying them into your article. Other finishing touches may also be added at this stage: the headline, the subhead and miscellaneous elements such as "pull quotes" or "blurbs." These are the large-type excerpts from your article used on later pages to help catch the reader's eye.

The magazine is coming together, and your article is one of many pieces in the puzzle. A dummy layout for the whole magazine—all the ads, all the articles—will be prepared. Your editor, looking at the completed dummy, now sees that the last column of your article will be sharing a page with an ad for a new dog mouthwash. Sorry, you don't have any say in the matter and your editor may not either.

STEP 6: PUBLICATION DAY

An immutable law of the magazine universe is that a writer is almost always the last person to see his or her article in print. Your cousin stationed at a remote naval base in Antarctica will probably see it before you do.

If the magazine you're writing for is sold on newsstands, start looking for a copy toward the end of the month before its cover date. To have a longer shelf life, most magazines come out ahead of the date on their covers. A November issue, for example, will usually appear during the last week in October and sometimes even earlier. Subscribers may get their copies before that.

Once the magazine is out, the freelancer's job may still not be finished. If the magazine has an enterprising publicity department, you may be asked to do radio or TV interviews timed to coincide with the issue's release. Publicity appearances can be flattering and fun. They may even put you back in touch with old friends. But remember, they also take you away from your writing.

With any luck, you're busy with another assignment by now, maybe several of them. But before you file that just-published article away in your archives, give it one last look. If you sold only first or one-time rights, you may be able to sell it to another magazine.

Meanwhile, behind the scenes at the magazine: When the issue containing your article finally appears, it may already seem like ancient history to the staff of the magazine. They've probably sent the next issue to the printer and are hard at work on the one or two after that.

All of which means that the magazine is open to new article proposals from you. So, brave freelancer: To arms!

2 SELLING WHAT YOU WRITE

"Study the magazine."

That may be the most clichéd advice ever offered to people who want to write for magazines. It may also be the best.

If you wanted to work for, say, a steel mill, you'd do what you could to learn about the kind of steel it made, try to get its annual report and so forth. But with a magazine, everything is there in black and white and a lot of other colors.

For most of your life you've probably read magazines. But unless you've been writing professionally, you've read them like a reader. In this chapter we'll look at how to read a magazine like a writer—a writer who wants to sell it something. The process, as you'll see, can be very different.

THE COVER

What a magazine puts on its cover can tell you a lot about who it thinks its readers are and what it believes they're interested in. Does it favor articles about health, money, travel, sex, relationships? Does it seem to be addressing men, women or both? Young readers or older ones? Does it treat its material seriously or with a sense of humor?

Consider these two cover lines on the subject of cordless screwdrivers from the magazines *Consumer Reports* and *Verge*. "Screwdrivers"—*Consumer Reports*. "Screw anywhere"—*Verge*. Which magazine do you think fancies itself a title for hip young men?

THE TABLE OF CONTENTS

Somewhere, usually in the first dozen pages of the magazine, will be a list of its entire fare for that issue. Reading it will give you a more rounded picture of what the magazine wants than its cover alone will. Here, for example, you'll see whether the magazine runs personal essays—a genre unlikely to make it to the magazine's cover but possibly a regular part of its mix nonetheless.

Here, too, you'll usually see bylines. They can tell you whether the magazine leans heavily on big-name writers or is open to newcomers. A quick comparison of the bylines on the table of contents and the names of staffers listed on the masthead can tell you whether the magazine is largely staff written or freelance written. A contributors column, if the magazine has one, can give you further insight into what kind of writers that magazine generally uses.

THE MASTHEAD

Not every magazine has a masthead. *The New Yorker*, for example, is famous for not having one. When a magazine does list its staff, you can scan it for a likely name to address your query to. Here are some of the job titles you're likely to see, starting at the top:

Editor in chief (sometimes just Editor)—the person in charge of the editorial part of the magazine. Except on magazines with very small staffs, the editor in chief may not work directly with many writers, especially new ones. Sometimes, though, he or she is the best person to address a query to, since it's likely to be passed on to the appropriate editor.

Executive editor—another editor who may not work directly with many writers but may instead manage other editors.

Managing editor—often an editor in charge of getting the magazine out on schedule. Some managing editors work with freelance writers, but most in my experience, don't.

Articles editor—pretty much what it sounds like. The articles editor, if the magazine has one, is often the best person to address your query to.

Senior editor, associate editor, assistant editor, etc.—editors with varying degrees of authority who may or may not work with freelance writers. Sometimes an editor who is relatively low on the masthead will be a good bet because he or she may take more interest in you than more experienced editors who are already working with as many writers as they can handle. Other times,

11

junior editors will simply be too preoccupied with advancing their own careers to show much interest in yours. So you take your chances.

THE DEPARTMENTS

The biggest difference between departments and articles is their length. Departments run shorter pieces—often much shorter ones. While a full-length article may run 2,000 words or longer, a department may only be 750 to 1,000 words. So if you're interested in writing short pieces, study the departments, which you'll usually find in the front and back of the magazine. Here are a few questions to ask as you do:

- What are the regular departments in the magazine, and what subject area does each one cover?
- Do they appear to be written by regular columnists or open to a variety of writers?
- Are the writers on staff (check the masthead) or freelance?

THE ARTICLES

Articles often appear in what's referred to as a "well," more or less in the middle of the magazine. Some magazines open their wells with that issue's cover story. Others simply start with any article that seems appropriate. Either way, when the little departments in the front of the magazine end (and before the little ones in the back begin), you'll typically find the magazine's longest features, often page after glossy page of them, uninterrupted by ads. What can you learn from the articles you find there? Here are a few things:

- How does the magazine usually begin its articles? With an anecdote? With the latest news on the subject? Or with some other type of lead? (For the lowdown on leads, see chapter six.)
- Does it run any essays or pieces written in the first person?
- Does it like humor?
- Does it often use sidebars?
- Does it run seasonal articles?
- How long are its articles, in general? (To get a quick estimate, count the words in an average paragraph and multiply by the number of paragraphs.)

Ideally, you should go through this process with at least two or three recent issues of your target magazine. But if all you can scrounge up is a single copy, you can still get a clue to what past issues have covered by reading the letters to the editor, if the magazine prints any. Many magazines also run a box with short blurbs about future articles, which can give you a hint of what's coming up.

THE ADVERTISING

Yes, you can even learn something from a magazine's advertising. Thomas Clark, former editor of *Writer's Digest*, notes that the products in ads offer a lot of clues to the kinds of people who are reading the magazine. For example, says Clark, "Are we talking about a 30-something urbanite who is single or a 40-year-old midwestern housewife with two kids?"

So even if you normally whiz past the ads, give them a look. A magazine stuffed with pitches for expensive watches, luxury automobiles and pricey perfumes probably goes to a wealthier audience than one whose advertisers are promoting economy cars and canned soup. A magazine with ads for baby diapers presumably reaches younger readers than one with ads for the adult kind.

WRITER'S GUIDELINES

You can also glean some of the above information by sending for the writer's guidelines many magazines offer in return for a self-addressed, stamped envelope. The problem with guidelines is that they're often out of date; magazines change quickly these days, and revising their editorial guidelines is seldom a high priority.

Can you learn anything of use from guidelines? Sometimes. A magazine's guidelines may, for example, tell you how far ahead it works. That can be helpful if you're hoping to propose an article that should run at a specific time of year. The guidelines may also tell you whether the magazine wants you to supply photos and, if so, what format it prefers.

Perhaps most useful of all, guidelines often tell you what the magazine is *not* interested in. For example, the guidelines for *Smithsonian Magazine* note that, "We do not consider fiction, poetry, travel features, political and news events, or previously published articles." *Popular Mechanics* magazine's guidelines tell would-be automotive writers that, "We do all of our own road testing and conduct our own owner surveys. Please don't query us about submitting driving reports on specific models or articles about what it's like to own a specific car."

THE MAGAZINES MOST OPEN TO NEW WRITERS

Some magazines are more receptive to new writers than others. Here are five types of publications that are almost always looking for fresh talent:

1. New magazines. Some eight hundred to nine hundred new magazines are launched each year, according to Samir A. Husni, a University of Mississippi journalism professor who compiles an annual guide to new magazines. Half will fail within a year, Husni says, and only three of every ten will still be in business after four years. But while they are around, they'll need writers—and lots of them.

New magazines are especially receptive to new writers for a couple of reasons. One, obviously, is that they don't have a vast network of writers in place yet. Another is that new magazines usually don't have the editorial budgets of larger ones, so they're often willing to take a chance on less-experienced (in other words, cheaper) writers.

How do you find out about new magazines before they're old magazines? The easiest way is to keep checking both your local newsstand and the supermarket magazine racks for titles you've never seen before.

Another good source of information on new magazines and ones still on the drawing board are the trade magazines that people in the publishing business read. Among the most useful are *Advertising Age*, *Adweek* and *Folio: The Magazine for Magazine Management*. *Writer's Digest* can also tip you off to new magazines. So, on occasion, will *The Wall Street Journal* and the business sections of *The New York Times* and other major newspapers.

And never underestimate the value of your own mailbox. What may be mere junk mail to your neighbors could be valuable information to you. Years ago I received a mailing from *Yankee* magazine, announcing a new spin-off called *Collectibles Illustrated*. I wrote to the editor of the new magazine, enclosed some clippings of articles I'd done and offered my services in case he ever needed

14

a correspondent where I lived. Within weeks I had an assignment, and over the next three years, until the magazine's untimely demise, I wrote more than a dozen pieces.

2. Old magazines with new owners. When a magazine gets a new owner, things tend to change. A new owner almost inevitably means a new team of editors and, sometimes, a new approach to whatever the magazine covers. Any change of that sort means an opportunity for writers.

The best way to keep track of ownership changes is to read the trade magazines mentioned previously. Another is to take note when a magazine alters its logo or overall design. A new design may mean a new art director, another near inevitability after an ownership change.

3. Magazines that are changing frequency. A magazine expanding from six issues a year to twelve may need twice as much editorial material to fill its pages. Even a magazine going from ten issues a year to twelve may need twenty percent more. Any frequency boost is likely to mean the magazine is more open to new writers. Again, it pays to check those trade publications now and then and to watch the newsstands like a pro.

4. Magazines that are changing focus. Sometimes magazines take a new direction even without changing owners. That, too, may spell opportunity, since not all of the magazine's current writers will be right for the new and improved model.

5. Small magazines. Whether they're under new management or have been run by the same family since the War of 1812, small-circulation magazines tend to be more open to new writers than their giant competitors. Small magazines also tend to have smaller budgets, which means they often have to take talent where they find it. You may never make a living by writing for small magazines, but they can be a terrific place to gain some experience and accumulate a few good clips. What's more, the editors who work for small magazines often move on to bigger magazines as their own careers progress, taking their best writers along with them.

DO YOU NEED AN AGENT?

If you're not a salesperson by nature, you may love the idea of delegating the job of selling your articles—in other words, a literary

Editorial Etiquette in Five Easy No-Nos

The writer/editor relationship, alas, is rarely an equal one. Editors can often get away with being rude to writers, but writers don't get anywhere unless they're perfectly polite in return. The rules change once you're famous, of course. But in the meantime, here are five rules any writer would do well to heed:

No-No 1: Don't phone unless you're invited to. You could be interrupting crucial work or just ruining a lusty daydream. Either way, the editor is likely to be less open-minded about whatever you called to discuss than if you had put it on paper. Editors are better at dealing with paper anyway. (More about this in chapter three.)

No-No 2: Don't fax, either. The magazine could be waiting for a last-minute article or an urgent take-out menu.

No-No 3: Don't miss any deadlines you agree to. By the same token, don't agree to any deadlines you couldn't possibly make.

No-No 4: Don't complain about the difficulty of the assignment, the lousy pay or whatever. Editors won't hesitate to annoy you, but that doesn't mean you're allowed to annoy them.

No-No 5: Don't try to build up your work by making fun of something the magazine published. Sure, that last article on your favorite topic may have gotten all the facts wrong. But if you point that out, the editor may take it personally. Believe it or not, underneath their tough hides, editors can be very sensitive creatures.

agent. Unfortunately, agents rarely handle magazine work anymore, preferring instead to concentrate on books, where the pay (and their 10 or 15 percent cut of it) tends to be better. When you're ready to write books, a reputable agent can be enormously helpful in selling your work. In the magazine market, though, plan on being your own sales rep. You may even find, as quite a few writers do, that you come to enjoy the selling nearly as much as the writing.

3 WHERE TO GET GREAT IDEAS

More than paper, more than ink, more even than those annoying subscription cards that tumble out at every opportunity, magazines are made of ideas.

Behind every magazine is an idea. Behind every article within the magazine is an idea. Behind every sentence within an article is—or darn well ought to be—an idea.

And where do all those ideas come from? Many come from writers.

Thinking up salable article ideas is a skill that some lucky writers may be born with but that most, I believe, develop over time. When you are first starting out as a writer, you may worry that you'll run out of ideas any day now. By the time you've been at it for a few years, you'll be producing more ideas than you'll ever be able to use.

SIX WAYS TO GENERATE MORE IDEAS

1. Take a lot of showers. Ask any twenty successful freelance writers where they get their best ideas, and I'll bet nineteen of them will say, "in the shower." There's even some science to back them up—something about negative ions, as I recall. But who cares, as long as it works? Keep your brain focused on story ideas rather than letting it wander all over the place. Otherwise you may waste whole showers making grocery lists or thinking up new ways to clean the shower curtain.

2. Put your subconscious to work. Remember that one writer in twenty who doesn't get ideas in the shower? Odds are he or she would tell you that the best ideas seem to bubble up out of nowhere. That, some say, is the subconscious mind at work. You don't have to sit back and wait for your subconscious to start bubbling, either. You can give it an assignment. That, anyhow, was the claim of Napoleon Hill, one of the founders of *Success* magazine. Once, when Hill was trying to come up with a title for a new book, he had a little talk with his subconscious before he went to bed. "I've got to have a million-dollar title, and I've got to have it tonight," he said. (And he said it out loud, yet.) "Do you understand that?"

Apparently his subconscious got the message, because at 2 A.M., Hill woke up, bounded to his typewriter and banged out the title. Hill's book, *Think and Grow Rich*, went on to sell more than twenty million copies and remains in print to this day.

When I've tried Hill's technique, the results have been mixed. Some mornings I'll wake up with an idea I've asked for. Other days I'll wake up with a good idea but on an entirely different subject. The rest of the time I just wake up.

Since your subconscious has a mind of its own and can spit out ideas any hour of the day or night, keep pen and paper in your pocket, in your car, on your night stand and any other place a brainstorm is likely to strike.

3. Read everything you can get your hands or eyes on. The best writers I know not only try to keep up with the fields they cover but read just about anything in sight. Few of the things you read will pay off in an immediate story, but they all help feed that mysterious idea machine in your head.

Books. Poke around the library. Let yourself get lost in unfamiliar aisles. Check out the new releases at your local bookstore. Many of the freshest ideas these days appear first as book titles, then make their way into magazines.

Magazines. Read the ones you want to write for, of course, but look at others, too. You'll learn some new things and maybe discover new ways to tell a story. And you may even surprise yourself and stumble on a promising market or two.

Old magazines are another good source of idea fodder. Check out some of the great magazines of yore someday when you're in the library and have nothing else to do: *Holiday, Look, Saturday Review*, to name a few. Beware, though: You can waste a lot of time in the old magazine stacks, reliving other writers' past glories when you could be at the keyboard creating your own.

Newspapers. Your local paper can be a terrific source of article ideas, especially if it's not a paper that magazine editors regularly follow like *The New York Times.* You may see a story in your local paper that's ripe for telling practically as is in a national magazine. More often, though, you'll find hints of a possible national story. It may be a local trend that's yet to be widely written about or a local person whose tale could be one of several in an article reported from a national perspective. So keep your scissors handy. When you travel, scoop up the local papers there, too.

On-line. The Internet may be the both the biggest time-saver and the biggest time-waster ever invented. I've found it an incredibly useful research tool but seldom discover any worthwhile article ideas, no matter how many hours I spend browsing. One possible exception: Web sites sponsored by local newspapers; they're rarely as rich in detail as the papers themselves, but they offer a window on the goings-on in different parts of the country. And also unlike the papers themselves, they're mostly free (at least as of this writing).

4. Listen up. I find some of the best story ideas come from listening to my friends, neighbors and coworkers talk about their concerns of the moment. Magazines pay a lot of money to convene so-called "focus groups" of everyday people who sit around for an hour talking about their likes, dislikes and whatever else they're asked to discuss. You can accomplish much the same thing for free by paying attention when someone starts griping about X, singing the praises of Y or asking why no magazine has ever told the truth about Z.

For example, I once heard one of my neighbors asking another about the best way to send money to a family member traveling overseas. Until that moment, I'd never given the matter much thought. But I checked it out, and a few months later not only did I know the answer but several million magazine readers did as well.

5. Tap into your own experience. Forget for a moment that you're a writer. What's on your mind, just as a human being? If you've wondered about something, chances are other people have, too. The difference is, you're a writer and can go out, investigate the matter and maybe even get paid for coming back with the answer.

The beauty of your own personal experience is that it's forever changing. Have a baby, and you'll find yourself jotting down child-related story ideas. Switch jobs, change homes, get a divorce, get a disease, win a trip for two to exotic Bora Bora—all of life's amazing twists and turns can supply you with fresh ideas.

My friend Steve Fishman turned a brain hemorrhage into an award-winning magazine article, then into a widely acclaimed book called *A Bomb in the Brain*. I know at least three writers who have gotten stories out of the aggravation they went through after their wallets were stolen.

I'm not saying to lose your wallet or to lust after any other sort of misfortune. But do remember that the events of your life—the good ones and the bad ones—are all part of your material as a writer.

6. Get to know some PR people. Public relations men and women often have great ideas for stories before anybody else does. Many of them are former magazine or newspaper writers themselves. The trouble, of course, is that it's their job to put a spin on the idea that benefits their clients. The other trouble is that they're out to get their clients as much positive publicity as possible, so if you got their story tip, a few dozen other writers probably did, too. That said, I've found PR people worth paying attention to over the years. If nothing else, they can sometimes get you access to key experts and provide background information that you'd otherwise spend a lot of time digging up on your own. Just remember that their agendas and yours aren't identical.

WILL EDITORS SWIPE YOUR IDEAS?

Beginning writers often ask if magazines will steal their ideas. The best answer I can think of: Maybe, but it's not worth worrying about.

In more than twenty years as an editor, I have never stolen an idea from a writer—and I don't think I'm necessarily a shoo-in for sainthood. And in my twenty years as a writer, no magazine has ever stolen an idea of mine (as far as I know, anyhow).

Yes, I've heard a few horror stories along the way, but I don't think idea theft is a crime to lose a whole lot of sleep over. For one thing, a good writer is always generating ideas—far more than he or she can begin to use. For another, if a magazine wants to steal your idea, there is not much you can do about it.

I've seen writers try, though. Some are deliberately vague in their queries, hoping to tease the editor into giving them the assignment simply on faith. Others practically make editors sign formal nondisclosure agreements. All a writer really accomplishes by such amateur legal tactics is to insult the editor's integrity—a dumb marketing move if there ever was one.

Occasionally you'll see an idea you pitched to a magazine (and the magazine threw back) appear in that very magazine a month, a year or a decade later. Did somebody swipe your idea? Possibly, but more likely the idea came from another writer with a somewhat different approach. Few ideas are so unusual that only one writer will think of them. So chalk it up to coincidence or to just being ahead of your time. (And maybe avoid that magazine in the future.) Then move on. You'll probably have better ideas tomorrow anyway.

WHAT TO DO WITH AN IDEA ONCE YOU HAVE ONE

Ideas are the writer's raw material. And like any other raw material, they're far more valuable once they've been refined.

The most common problem that beginning writers seem to have is grasping the difference between a story idea and what's simply an interesting subject. Here's an illustration: Undersea exploration is an interesting subject, but it's way too broad for a magazine article.

You might, however, be able to sell a piece on how undersea exploration is raising some tough new ethical questions. For example, is the wreck of the *Titanic* fair game for souvenir hunters or a sacred resting place for its victims?

One useful test is to try to write a headline for your proposed article. If it sounds like a book title or a fourteen-part PBS series, you need to bring your idea into sharper focus. But if it sounds like a headline you might see in a magazine—particularly in the magazine you want to propose it to—you're probably on track.

HOW EDITORS LOOK AT YOUR IDEAS

You can boost your ideas' odds of success if you learn to step back and look at them the way an editor does. Not all editors think alike, of course, but if you could cut an editor's head open (and wouldn't we all like to sometimes?), you'd probably see a thought process that works something like this:

1. **"Does this idea belong in this magazine?"** Sometimes the answer is pretty obvious: A magazine about dogs probably won't be interested in a story about cats. Other times, it's far more subtle. A dog magazine that last year ran a story called "Rottweilers: Those Gentle Giants" is an unlikely market for your proposed piece on "Rottweilers: Four-Legged Psychopaths From Hell."

What can you do? Look up what the magazine has run in the past year or two in the *Readers' Guide to Periodical Literature* or on a computerized magazine database at your library. Not all magazines are indexed in this way, but some surprisingly obscure ones are. If you can't find out whether your idea conflicts with one the magazine has already done, just give it a shot. There's no shame in approaching a magazine with an idea that's just slightly off the mark.

2. **"Have we done this story before?"** And if so, how recently? Some magazines will return to the same topic month after month, as long as they can put at least the illusion of a fresh spin on it. Some women's magazines, for example, run a diet story in every issue, for the simple reason that such stories, however unbelievable, sell copies. Other magazines won't touch a topic that they've covered in the past five or ten years.

3. **"Have our competitors already done the story?"** Even if the magazine itself hasn't touched the topic, an editor may consider the idea old stuff if one or more of the magazine's competitors has. Magazines differ considerably in what they consider their competition. Some will look only to their specific category (boating magazines, decorating magazines, teen magazines and so forth), while others will consider newspapers, television and every other type of media. Generally speaking, you stand the best chance with ideas that have received no coverage or only very local coverage.

4. **"Is this the best way to approach this story?"** Sometimes a fresh approach can inject life into a tired topic. For example, "Six Ways to Childproof Your Home" would be a familiar approach to most editors of parenting magazines. But something like "How Professional Childproofers Rip You Off" or "Childproof Accessories That Could Injure Your Child" might get their attention.

5. **"Is this the best writer for the job?"** As I said earlier, magazines will seldom steal your ideas. But in some cases they may turn a

Exercise: Imagine Your Own Magazine

If you want to think like an editor, what better way than to start your own magazine? Since launching a real magazine costs something like $5 million a year for the first five years, last I heard, we'll do this exercise on paper. If you happen to have $25 million lying around, go ahead and try it for real.

Begin by asking yourself some questions:

What is your magazine about? What's its title? What's on the cover?

Who are your readers? How old are they? Are they men or women or both? (Or boys or girls, or both?)

Who is your competition? What will your magazine do that other magazines already out there don't?

Now, here's the fun part:

Make at least three sample tables of contents for your magazine. Figure you'll have six or seven feature stories and a similar number of regular departments in each issue.

As you list your feature stories, ask yourself if there are good sidebar possibilities. What about charts or tables? Try to picture the story laid out in the magazine. How many pages is it? How is it illustrated?

Once you have set down your ideas for articles and departments, you'll probably notice some overlaps or other conflicts between the different pieces. Can one of them be refocused to eliminate the problem? Or could it be switched with a piece on one of your other tables of contents?

By doing this exercise, you'll see how the tricky puzzle that is a magazine comes together. And you should have a better idea of how your work as a writer fits into that puzzle.

perfectly fine idea down if you don't seem like the right writer. In rare instances, they may offer to buy the idea from you and assign it to another writer.

What may make you inappropriate? Distance is one thing. If you come across a great story in Australia, but you happen to live in Albuquerque, the magazine may not have the budget to send you there. Or, if you are obviously a beginning writer, the magazine may hesitate to assign you what's sure to be a complex, ambitious story.

A magazine is most likely to take a chance on you if an editor there has worked with you elsewhere or knows your work from other publications. A powerful query and strong clips can also make a difference.

6. "Even if this idea isn't right, is the writer someone worth encouraging?" Some editors are too busy or too self-important to send personal notes to writers whose ideas may have just missed the mark. So don't automatically assume the worst if you receive a terse form letter in reply. Other editors will suggest a way an idea might be reshaped or urge you to try again with another one. If your query is impressive enough, an editor may come back at you with a story idea of his or her own.

4 WRITING QUERIES THAT WORK

The query letter can be your best sales tool. Indeed, it had better be. The morning mail at most magazines brings a pile of queries, and only a couple of them (if any) are likely to result in an assignment.

How do you make your query stand out from the pack? There's no surefire formula, no easy, fill-in-the-blanks query letter I or anybody else could provide to guide you. Even terrific queries can fail to work sometimes. Maybe it's because the magazine just assigned a similar piece, because its inventory of articles is overflowing or because the editor is simply in a mean mood that day.

But a good query at least has a chance, while a poor one doesn't have a prayer. In this chapter we'll look at some ways to write a good query—and to not write a bad one.

QUERY

A query really has two jobs. It must sell your idea, and it must sell you. Of those two jobs, selling you is far more important. An editor who likes your idea but doesn't like you probably won't give you an assignment. An editor who likes you but not the idea may assign you a different piece or at least urge you to try again.

So, how do you sell yourself? First, as your mean old third-grade teacher probably told you, neatness counts. Did you get the editor's name right? How about the magazine's? (Believe it or not, lots of would-be writers don't.) Did you check and recheck everything else in your letter—spelling, grammar, facts? Did you get your letter into the envelope without spilling coffee or Oreo crumbs on it?

Though most editors I know try to give query letters a fair shake, after reading them day in and day out, even the most open-minded editor begins to look for reasons to say no, rather than yes. A no at least gets the letter off the editor's desk, while a yes or a maybe means it will require more thinking. So don't give an editor an easy reason to say no.

Let's assume your letter is, well, letter-perfect. Now, what else does it say about you? Is it lively or dull? Thorough or sketchy? Logically organized or scattered? Fair or not, all the editor has to judge you on is your query.

STRUCTURING YOUR QUERY

As a magazine editor, I have seen queries of one paragraph and others of twenty pages or more. (One or two single-spaced pages usually does the job.) But whatever their length, most good queries are structured along these lines:

1. Editor's name and address
2. The sales pitch
3. Your credentials for writing the piece

Editor's name and address. It may seem a little weird to bring this one up, but I've been amazed over the years at how many freelancers sabotage their query before it gets started—just by the way they address it. For example, many writers will address a query simply to "Editor." That looks lazy, and as a result the letter tends to get about as much attention as one addressed to "Occupant." If you don't know the editor's name, a quick call to the magazine is worth your trouble. As mentioned back in chapter two, the editor in chief or articles editor will often be your best query target.

The sales pitch. Here's where you tell the editor what you want to write about. Many writers like to begin their queries with a lead, perhaps the same one they'd use on the article itself:

"Joe and Edna own a house so much like their next door neighbor's that they've often pulled into the wrong driveway by mistake. They used to laugh about it, until recently when they made a startling discovery. Joe and Edna's property taxes are more than four times as high as their neighbor's.

"For a host of reasons, many Americans are paying more than they should in local property taxes. I'd like to show your readers how they can successfully challenge their tax assessments and save hundreds of dollars every year."

Other writers are more direct:

"Experts say that more than twenty million Americans are over-paying on their local property taxes. I'd like to propose an article that will show your readers how they can determine whether their tax bills are too high and—if they are—to fight back and win."

Which way is better? It doesn't much matter, as long as your query gets the editor's attention and quickly explains why his or her readers will be interested in the article.

After describing the gist of the piece, you might want to elaborate a bit and mention any ideas you have for sidebars, graphs, tables, photos or whatever. In other words, try to give the editor a picture of the whole package that you could provide.

Even if you already know your subject, it almost always pays to do some fresh research before you write a query. That shows the editor that you can bring something new to the topic. But don't overdo it. You can waste a lot of time researching a topic only to discover that no magazine is interested or that some other writer got a query in ahead of you.

Try to be enthusiastic about any idea you propose. Enthusiasm, or the lack of it, is easy to detect in a query. If you aren't sold on an idea, you can't expect an editor to be. Plus, if you aren't genuinely enthusiastic about your idea but somehow get the assignment any-way, you'll probably wish you'd never gotten yourself into it.

In some cases, you'll want to close the pitch part of your letter with a sentence on how quickly you could deliver the piece. (For example, "I could have the finished piece on your desk within a month after assignment.") Monthly magazines usually work at least two months ahead, and in some cases even longer than that. So if you're proposing a piece that has something to do with Halloween for a monthly magazine's October issue (which probably comes out in September), you had better have your query in the mail by the end of June and be prepared to deliver by late July.

The writer's credentials. Mentioning other magazines you've written for can help sell both you and your idea. Editors take comfort in the fact that you've delivered the goods for other magazines, especially ones they've heard of. First-hand experience with whatever you're hoping to write about is often a plus and sometimes essential; if you're proposing a piece on challenging your property taxes and happen to have done that successfully yourself, mention it in your query letter. An advanced degree in the field you want to write about can sometimes help, too, as long as you can convince an editor that you know how to write for popular audiences and not just scholarly ones.

If you haven't published a lot of articles and don't have any other special credentials to offer, you can try a couple of things. One is to say nothing about your background and hope your idea is strong enough to succeed on its own merits. The other is to say up front that you're just getting started as a magazine writer. Some editors will take a chance on a new writer if they sense the person has talent and energy. Most editors can remember when they were new at the game, too. And just look at how they turned out. . . .

You may even want to consider volunteering to write the article "on spec." Spec is short for speculation, and writing on spec means the magazine won't owe you any money if the piece doesn't work out. Most experienced writers cringe—and rightly so—at the idea of writing on spec. But when you're just starting out, it can be one way to break in and collect some clips.

P.S.: Never underestimate the value of a good P.S. at the end of your query letter. People will often read a postscript even if they skip the rest of the letter.

Finally, keep copies of all your old query letters and go back through them every so often. Save them on your computer, if you have one, for easy retrieval. Some story ideas that didn't sell the first time around may simply have been ahead of their time. So if you're still enthusiastic about an idea, dust it off, update it as needed and get that sucker back into the mail.

THE MULTIPLE-IDEA QUERY

Some writers like to save time and a few stamps by proposing several article ideas in each query. That can work, as long as you develop the ideas fully enough so the editor can understand where you're headed. I wouldn't try to propose more than two or three ideas per query, though, or you'll end up with a very long letter.

One advantage to this approach is that it gives an editor you haven't worked with before a more rounded picture of you and your interests than any single idea would. The downside, as a very shrewd freelancer I know once explained to me, is that editors will tend to skim off the best idea in each group and turn down all the others. So perfectly fine ideas that might have sold, had they been the lone subject of a query, end up being rejected.

AND NOW, FOUR THINGS YOU DON'T WANT TO DO

1. Don't overpromise for the sake of an assignment. For example, don't promise an interview with some famously reclusive movie star unless you are reasonably sure you can make it happen. Don't promise a first-person piece on ballooning over the Alps if you're afraid of heights. And don't promise to play the world's ten toughest miniature golf courses unless you have the time to do it. If you can't deliver the story you promise in your query, you may embarrass yourself, alienate the editor who took a chance on you and dash any hopes of future assignments.

2. Don't mess with simultaneous submissions. Some books on magazine writing suggest that you send the same query at the same time to different magazines, a tactic known as a "simultaneous submission." Not this book. In my experience, simultaneous submissions are usually a bad idea. They may seem efficient, in that you won't have to wait for magazine A's verdict before you can send the idea to magazine B. But they will turn off most editors, who would prefer to think you have your heart set on wooing them and them alone. Imagine asking someone to marry you and casually mentioning that you're also asking several other people, just in case.

You *could* send out simultaneous submissions without mentioning that fact. However, if the various editors find out (and they may, especially if more than one magazine ends up being interested in the idea), they may feel you were trying to hoodwink them.

3. Don't send photocopied queries. They almost always lead to photocopied rejection slips. A photocopied query looks cheap and makes the editor wonder how many magazines have already passed on it. Editors like to feel that any idea you bring to them is fresh and original, not something other editors have seen and rejected. If you have a computer with a printer, it's easy to run out a fresh copy each time you want to send a proposal to a different magazine. Otherwise, plan to do a lot of retyping.

4. Don't query by phone—unless you have a truly hot and timely idea. If you've discovered that Amelia Earhart is waiting tables in your local diner—and nobody else knows about it—many editors would be happy to talk to you. Otherwise, use paper.

And I don't mean fax paper. Faxed queries are nearly as annoying as phone calls. The magazine may have more urgent uses for its fax machine, such as last-minute corrections from writers working on assigned pieces. I have known several major magazines that had just one or two fax machines to serve their entire editorial departments. Faxed queries are also ineffective for another reason: Editors don't know what to do with them. A letter seems to invite another letter in response, and freelancers often include a self-addressed, stamped envelope for that purpose. But what does an editor do with a fax? Reply by fax (and tie up the machine all the more)? Reply by letter? Or just give up and throw the fax away? The only time it really makes sense to query by fax is if an editor has invited you to. Even then you may want to send a second copy by letter, just in case your fax gets swept into somebody else's pile of papers.

Then, of course, there is E-mail, or (if somebody else hasn't claimed the word yet) E-queries. On the annoyance scale, E-queries would rank somewhere below unsolicited phone calls and faxes—but just barely. An unsolicited E-mail is an intrusion on an editor's time, though one that's easier to answer (or just delete) than most other forms of correspondence. The etiquette of E-mail is still in the formative stages, but for now I'd advise not cluttering an editor's electronic mailbox unless you've been invited to.

WHEN TO SKIP THE QUERY

There are certain kinds of magazine pieces that editors will tell you they need to see in their entirety before they can make a decision. These tend to be pieces where the telling is as important as what's being told. Essays based on a personal experience often fall into this category, as do fiction and humor. An editor can usually fix up a bad how-to piece, for example. A humor piece is either funny or it isn't, and there isn't much an editor can do about it.

The conventional wisdom is that if you want to write such pieces, plan to send in a finished manuscript rather than a query. My experience, however, is that it sometimes pays to query even in these instances. For one thing, an editor can tell you whether he or she is interested in such a piece, before you've spent hours and hours writing and polishing it. For another—and this is the important one—an editor's invitation to send the piece should mean that it will get more careful consideration than it might otherwise.

TO SASE OR NOT TO SASE

It's traditional in the magazine business for writers to enclose a self-addressed, stamped envelope with their queries. Indeed, many publications expect you to and even mention it in their writer's guidelines and their listings in *Writer's Market*. Never mind that more and more magazines these days are owned by billion-dollar corporations and ought to be able to afford a little postage.

Some writers deliberately don't enclose SASEs with their queries. They think a SASE makes it far too easy for an editor to return a query without giving it proper consideration. All the editor (or more likely, the editor's assistant) has to do is attach a rejection slip or scribble something at the bottom of the query, pop it into that envelope, and good-bye. Another anti-SASE argument I've heard in recent years is that a query from a professional writer to an editor is business correspondence and deserves a reply, SASE or no.

So what do you do? Personally, I'd enclose a SASE unless I had already written for that magazine or that editor long enough to establish an ongoing relationship. Enclosing a SASE may well make it easy for an editor to reject your query, but if you don't enclose one, he or she may simply throw it away, leaving you wondering whether the magazine got it to begin with. Some editors throw away unsolicited queries SASE and all, of course, and some may even soak your stamps off to stick on their own mail; but most editors will use your envelope for the purpose you intended.

The SASE may be a dumb tradition, but as with lots of other dumb traditions, it's sometimes easier to go along with than to spend time fretting about. Consider, for example, the necktie.

5 A QUICK COURSE IN MANUSCRIPT MECHANICS

Entire books have been written on the exciting subject of preparing manuscripts for publication. Fortunately, you don't have to read any of them. For magazine writers, the rules are simple. This chapter will tell you what you need to know, so you can focus on more important things—like the writing itself.

FORGET FANCY

When you're trying to break into the magazine business, you may figure that fluorescent paper, a snazzy binder or a paper clip that plays "The Star-Spangled Banner" will make your manuscript stand out from the pack. Indeed, such gimmicks will help your work stand out—as the product of an amateur.

As far as I know, no editor has ever bought a manuscript because he or she liked the packaging. But many editors have, I suspect, turned down potentially publishable pieces because they *didn't* like it.

So how do you walk that fine line? First, keep things simple. Buy some 8½" × 11" typing or photocopying paper—white, not off-white or any other color. Either 16-lb. or 20-lb. paper (it says on the box) should be fine. Don't worry about cotton content—except maybe for your stationery, which we'll get to later.

If you use a typewriter, be sure the keys are clean and your ribbon has enough ink in it to make crisp black letters on the page. If you use a computer, aim for the same result. And if your computer happens to be of the old dot matrix variety, plan to trade up to a letter-quality model as soon as you have the cash. Many editors won't even read dot matrix manuscripts.

Set your margins to an inch or an inch and a half. Leave about four inches of white space at the top of the front page (except for your name and address). That gives the editor room to write a headline or typesetting instructions if, lucky you, your piece is purchased.

Your name, address and phone/fax numbers should go at the upper left of all that white space. Some writers put their social security numbers up there, too, in hopes of speeding up payment. But my advice is to keep that number to yourself until your editor or somebody in the magazine's accounting department asks you for it. In the wrong hands, your social security number can be a magic "open sesame" to all kinds of financial information and other stuff you're better off keeping private.

If you want, you can put a word count up there, too: "About 2,000 words," for example. Some editors appreciate it, while others pay no attention.

Double-space your type and number your pages. If you use a computer and haven't figured out how to number the pages automatically (it took me about twelve years), write the numbers in by hand. Use a paper clip rather than a staple to hold your manuscript together, just in case your editor hasn't had a tetanus shot lately.

BE ORIGINAL

For the sake of convenience, you may be tempted to send out a photocopy of a manuscript rather than an original that's been through your printer or typewriter. Bad idea.

A photocopied manuscript makes any editor wonder how many other magazines have already seen the piece and turned it down. If you use a computer, it's easy enough to run out a new copy. And if you use a typewriter, this may be reason enough to get a computer.

In the case of book manuscripts, photocopies may be OK. But for magazines, forget it.

SUBMITTING ELECTRONICALLY

If your piece is purchased, the editor may ask if you can send a copy electronically, either on a disk or by E-mail, so the magazine doesn't have to retype it. Be sure to ask what software programs the editors use; otherwise, your piece may come out at their end looking like hieroglyphics. Fortunately, the technology is a lot more forgiving than

YOU CAN WRITE FOR MAGAZINES

it used to be—allowing, for example, a magazine to convert articles written with one software program to be read by a computer using another.

When you send a computer disk, include a paper version of your manuscript (known these days as a "hard copy"). This is especially important if the magazine will be using a software program different from your own. In that case, some of the coding to indicate italics, boldface letters, underlining and so forth may be lost in the translation. Your paper manuscript can show the editors exactly what you intended.

Finally, if you do send a disk, don't count on getting it back. Odds are it will end up in a desk drawer or as a coaster under somebody's morning coffee. So don't leave any files on there that you can't afford to lose.

KEEP IT CLEAN

As with queries, neatness counts when you're preparing a manuscript. In fact, it probably counts more than ever now, since computers have made it so easy to catch and correct errors before they're ever printed out. A typewritten manuscript with even a couple of hand-corrected errors is at a serious disadvantage these days unless the editor already knows you and your work.

And while it may be needless to say, I'll say it anyway: Never send out a manuscript with coffee, food or who-knows-what kind of stains on it. Unbelievable as it may seem, I've seen more than a few of them in my time as a magazine editor. No manuscript that looks as if it should be handled with tongs has much chance of acceptance.

STATIONERY THAT SELLS

F. Scott Fitzgerald once had stationery printed up for himself that said:

F. Scott Fitzgerald
Hack Writer and Plagiarist
St. Paul, Minnesota

Tip: Don't do that. They might not know you're kidding.

The best advice on stationery, as with manuscripts, is to keep it simple. You might want to use somewhat swankier paper for your stationery, say 24-lb. paper with 25 percent cotton content. You can even be a bit bolder with color, trying off-white or ivory, for instance. Hey, you only go around once in life.

You can have your name and address professionally printed on the paper, do it yourself with your computer printer or simply type it on. As long as your stationery looks reasonably professional, as opposed to the work of a deranged crackpot, you'll be OK. If you have stationery printed, stick to a basic ink like blue or black. Brown ink on beige paper looked pretty good in the 1970s, but then again so did polyester.

So what should you call yourself? Some writers just use their names. Others strive mightily and often unsuccessfully to create a funny company name. A few years ago, the fad was names followed by Ink (rather, of course, than Inc.). The first one of those that an editor saw probably seemed sort of clever. The next few dozen seemed less and less so.

Aside from not overtaxing your creative powers, there's another good reason for simply going with whatever name your parents (or whoever) gave you. As your byline begins to appear here and there, you'll be building name recognition. And when a letter with your name on it—as opposed to a made-up company name—arrives on some harried editor's desk, he or she may pause and think, "Haven't I seen that name before?" That alone can save your letter from the recycling bin and at least give it a chance for a fair hearing.

Personally, I'd also avoid putting anything on your letterhead like "freelance writer," "professional writer," "wordsmith" or "member of the British Royal Family." Ditto for little cartoons of typewriters or quill pens meant to convey the idea that you're a writer. If your query or cover letter doesn't convince an editor that you're a real writer, nothing you can stick on your stationery will do the job for you.

Do, however, include on your letterhead your name, address and phone number, as well as any fax number or E-mail address. Anything that makes it easier for an editor to get in touch with you increases the odds that one may actually do so.

GIVE YOUR MANUSCRIPT A FINAL INSPECTION

As an editor, I've sometimes wished that when I opened a manuscript from a freelancer, one of those little INSPECTED BY NUMBER 123 slips would tumble out. That would give me some assurance that what I was about to read was as accurate as the writer could make it. As a writer, I've learned that however hard I've worked on a piece, a final inspection before I send it off almost always turns up something that I'm glad I caught before my editor could. Here's a five-point checklist for inspecting your manuscripts:

√ Are the names spelled right? Few mistakes are more embarrassing—or more preventable—than getting someone's name wrong. Even if the misspelling is caught by the publication's fact checkers and never slips into print, your reputation for accuracy will be trashed. In case you don't know, fact checkers love telling on writers.

To guard against misspellings, I always ask people I'm quoting to spell their names for me, then I write the names in my notes in big block letters. I also ask for a business card if the person seems likely to have one, but I never rely on clippings from other publications, even if my subject gave them to me. If you're ever in doubt, call your subject back. Some people may be irritated, but most of them will be grateful that you took the trouble.

√ Do the numbers add up? If you don't check your math, somebody else will—usually some smug reader who will proceed to use you as Exhibit A in his critique of the U.S. educational system. We're not talking quadratic equations here: Even the simplest numbers can get you into trouble. So if you write, "Here are six tips for ridding your garden of nasty pests," make sure you really list six tips, not five and not seven. I once wrote a piece on "50 Ways to Save $50 or More" and didn't notice until I was about to turn in the manuscript that one way had gone astray and I'd only listed forty-nine. Fortunately, I did notice in time to do something about it.

√ Are the phone numbers correct? The best way to check is to dial them yourself. And do it right before you turn your manuscript in, just in case they've recently changed.

√ Is everything else spelled right? The spell checkers that come with today's word-processing programs have made life a lot easier for those of us who wouldn't stand much chance in a spelling bee. But even if you use a spell checker, don't stop there. A spell checker is good for telling you that the word is *quandary* not *quandry*, or *maneuver* and not *manuver*, but it won't help you if you typed *their* when you meant *there* or *the* when you meant *then*. So give your manuscript an old-fashioned read before you send it on its way.

√ Check your quotes. Many publications will verify any quotes you use by reading them (or a paraphrase) back to the source. But don't count on it. I always check interview quotes against my notes or against my typed transcript if I taped the interview. For quotes I've taken from a book, I read my manuscript and the printed version side by side. (And between you and me, it's amazing how often I'll find an error—usually a minor one, fortunately—has crept in.) For various reasons, people may still accuse you of misquoting them, but at least you and your editor will know that you did a professional job.

One final tip: If you have time, let your manuscript sit for a day or two, then give it one last look. A couple of days' distance can be nearly as good as having your own INSPECTOR NUMBER 123 on the premises.

6 THE SECRETS OF WINNING LEADS

Some writers will tell you that a good magazine article lead should grab the reader by the throat. Others would rather describe it as a passionate first kiss.

But whether they fancy themselves fighters or lovers, experienced writers agree that crafting those first few sentences is one of the most important—and trickiest—parts of their trade. A sensational lead can sell an editor on buying and working with an otherwise iffy piece. A lousy lead can cause that same editor to lunge for a rejection slip—no matter how good the rest of the piece may be.

Unlike news reporters, who can fall back on the old who-what-when-where-why style of lead, magazine writers have no safe formulas to follow. But the veteran freelancers I know say there are, at least, a few loose guidelines. Following those guidelines can help make the difference between a sparkling lead and a dull one, a check or a "Sorry. . . ."

Where to begin? For lack of a better place, at the beginning:

KNOW THE MAGAZINE YOU'RE WRITING FOR
Yes, I know you've heard that one before. But it's nowhere more true than in the writing of leads. Call it style, tone, point of view, attitude or whatever, magazine editors want to approach every story, from word one, in their own unique way.

Magazines vary, too, in such basics as whether they prefer their leads long or short. *The New Yorker*, to choose a prominent example, has run leads longer than other magazines' entire articles.

And, above all else, magazines differ in their focus, even when they're writing about the very same thing. Consider two 1992 profiles of the comedian Jay Leno, who was then about to succeed Johnny Carson as host of the *Tonight Show*. While the two pieces reported many of the same facts, they started off in characteristically different ways.

Time magazine's Leno profile began not with the man himself, but with a description of his chair, the chair he would sit in when he took over from Carson. To *Time*, that chair was a throne, and the fact that Leno would soon be ascending to it made him *Time*-ly.

Woman's Day, in a Leno profile published around the same time as *Time*'s, took an entirely different approach. It led off with Leno's observations about different kinds of moms—a large part of the *Woman's Day* audience. The punch line: "I've got the kind of mom who irons socks."

If a cooking magazine profiled Leno, it would probably start with him fooling around in the kitchen. A magazine for automobile buffs might begin with him in his garage, showing off his collection of vintage cars and motorcycles.

Fortunately, it's easy enough to figure out how a particular magazine would like you to lead off your article. Read a few recent issues. If the editor hasn't changed since those issues came out, the magazine's approach will probably have remained pretty much the same. And if you're unsure, ask.

Joseph Anthony, a Portland, Oregon, writer who has freelanced for such magazines as *Better Homes and Gardens* and *National Geographic Traveler*, says he often asks editors for their thoughts on how an article should begin as soon as they assign him to write it. "That helps me focus me on what they think is important," he says. "It also forces them to focus on what it is they want."

KNOW THE *PART* OF THE MAGAZINE YOU'RE WRITING FOR

Just as magazines differ in their approaches to leads, so do the various sections within any one magazine. A department of short items at the front of the magazine may take an altogether different approach from the longer departments toward the back of the magazine. The feature-length articles in between may take still another approach.

Katy Koontz, a Knoxville, Tennessee, freelancer for such magazines as *Reader's Digest* and *Travel and Leisure*, says, "If you're writing shorts, for example, you usually can't lead with an anecdote. You won't have room for much else."

GET THE READER'S ATTENTION

Whatever magazine—and whatever section of it—you're writing for, never lose sight of the purpose of a lead. That's to get your reader to stop turning the pages and start reading your story.

"You have to remember that as writers we're all in the entertainment business," says freelancer Joseph Anthony. "You have to come out dancing as fast as you can."

His advice: "Home in on the thing that's most frightening or different about your subject. Try to personalize it for the reader. Show what one person has done, talk about one family's experiences."

The best leads, says freelancer Koontz, "make people who wouldn't normally be interested in your story read it. And for that you need something really wild: a great quote, an outrageous statement."

Once you've grabbed the reader, then what? Don't let go, advises Nancy Dunnan, a New York freelancer for such magazines as *Parents* and *Self*. Her favorite technique: a first-sentence grabber followed by a second sentence that tells the reader what the article will do for him or her. "Often it helps to attach a number to whatever you're writing about," Dunnan says. "For example, 'Here are twelve ways to invest' or 'Here are seven top hotels in Maine.' A number like that gives readers a feeling that they can conquer the material."

THINK TWICE BEFORE RECYCLING THE LEAD
OF YOUR QUERY AS THE LEAD OF YOUR STORY

Sometimes that works, but often your editor will have become bored with it by the time your manuscript arrives. If you use that lead again, he or she may take that as a sign of laziness or a lack of imagination. And neither of those impressions will do much for your writing career.

Most editors assume that when you send them a query you've done some preliminary research on your topic, but not much more than that. Once you receive an assignment, they expect you to really immerse yourself in your subject. In the course of your research, you'll often come across a better lead than the one in your query.

That doesn't mean, of course, that you should just blow off the lead of your query, figuring you'll come up with something catchy when the time comes to write the article. If your query doesn't sell the editor, you may never get that chance. Joseph Anthony approaches query leads this way: "The lead of your query should be what you *think* the lead of your story will be, before you've done your reporting. But when the time comes to write your story, you can't be wedded to it."

USE QUOTES SPARINGLY—AND CAREFULLY

It's tempting, particularly when you're writing a personality profile, to let your subject have the first word. That's usually a mistake. A sentence or two from you, setting up the quote, will establish right from the start that you, not your subject, are in control.

Quotes from people who figure in your story but aren't its principal focus can be even more troublesome. Steve Fishman, who has contributed to such magazines as *Details*, *GQ* and *Rolling Stone*, says using a quote in a lead almost always puts the writer at a disadvantage. "Leads have to set the tone for the story, establish the voice, tell you whether it's going to be an adventure that takes you along or a policy piece that lays out the issues involved," he says. "It's very hard to use someone else's words to do that."

RESIST THE URGE TO QUOTE SHAKESPEARE
OR MARK TWAIN

They didn't need to quote you.

Still, you may find inspiration for your leads in books of quotations. That's one of the places writer Nancy Dunnan turns to when she's stuck for a lead. More about getting stuck—and getting unstuck—a bit later.

AVOID CLICHÉS—UNLESS YOU CAN
PUT A NEW SPIN ON THEM

Don't be the millionth writer to say you have good news and bad news. Say you have good news and good news. Or good news and better news. Better still, forget good news and bad news. Start with something completely fresh.

Remember: If you've seen it before, your reader may have, too. And your editor almost certainly has.

Besides relying on your own cliché-hunting instincts, consider reading your lead aloud to a fellow writer, a friend, a spouse. They may be too kind to tell you that you've used a cliché, so watch for any telltale winces.

START A COLLECTION OF OTHER WRITERS' LEADS

Photographers and illustrators often maintain a "swipe file" filled with examples of how their fellow artists handled certain subjects. We writers, of course, can swipe with the best of them.

The point isn't to copy other writers' work, but to learn from their techniques, especially in tricky situations. How did they set up a quote? How did they introduce a setting? How did they make the transition from the lead paragraph to the rest of the article?

Steve Fishman says he sometimes types other writers' leads onto his computer screen and tries to take them apart, to see how they achieved a certain effect. Among his favorite lead writers: Joan Didion, Christopher Isherwood, V.S. Naipaul and Tom Wolfe.

You don't have to confine your swiping to writers who do the same sort of stuff you do. Nonfiction writers can learn a lot about leads from short-story writers. Magazine writers can pick up ideas from newspaper columnists and sportswriters. *The Wall Street Journal*, drab as it may look from a distance, is a model of colorful lead writing.

You can even learn something about lead writing from—gasp!—television. Geoffrey C. Ward, a New York writer who has freelanced for such magazines as *American Heritage* and *National Geographic* and who was also the principal writer of the acclaimed documentary series *The Civil War*, says, "Very good TV writing is very, very simple. I have learned how surprisingly few words are required. Writing for television shows you how conversational and terse you can be and still say quite a lot."

IF YOU'RE STUCK, SKIP THE LEAD
AND COME BACK TO IT LATER

When I wrote this section, I still hadn't written the lead for this chapter. Instead, I just wrote "Lead TK" (magazine jargon for "lead to come") and plunged in at the first major point I wanted to make. By the time you read this, of course, I'll have written a lead. (And, considering the subject matter, it better be a decent one.)

There are probably as many tricks for overcoming lead writer's block as there are writers. Eleanor Berman, a New York writer who has freelanced for such magazines as *Washingtonian* and *Working Mother*, says she often uses "an old headline writers' trick. I just sit down in front of a blank computer screen and write as many different leads as I can think of, one after another."

Nancy Dunnan, as I mentioned earlier, sometimes consults *Bartlett's Familiar Quotations* for inspiration. Almanacs, encyclopedias and books of historical dates can also be useful lead-inspirers, she says.

Longtime freelancer Hank Nuwer, however, says he can't write a piece until he has his lead down on paper. His solution: "Train yourself to spot a lead while doing your research. When someone I'm interviewing tells me a story that might serve as the perfect lead, I always jot a brief reminder in my research notes."

DON'T GET DISCOURAGED IF, AFTER YOU'VE
FOLLOWED ALL THE ADVICE ABOVE, SOME NASTY
EDITOR CHANGES YOUR LEAD ANYHOW

Here are two tales from my own experiences on both sides of the writer/editor barricades:

Once, as a writer, I was assigned by a magazine for teenagers to write a sidebar that would accompany another writer's article on rock concert photography. When the magazine appeared, I was happy to see that the lead I had labored so hard over was published exactly as I had written it. My happiness was tempered, however, by the fact that my lead was now atop the *other* writer's article and

YOU CAN WRITE FOR MAGAZINES

under *his* byline. As to my sidebar, the magazine ran it without any lead at all.

Some years later, as an editor at another magazine, I saw first-hand how bad things happen to good leads. Our art director decided, shortly before the magazine was to go on press, that a certain article would look far better on the page if it began with a large capital *H*. Unfortunately, that meant rewriting the freelance author's well-crafted lead, a crime that fell to me to commit. Yes, magazines work in mysterious ways.

DON'T FEEL OBLIGED TO RELATE THE END OF YOUR STORY BACK TO THE LEAD

That technique can work on very short pieces, but may seem strained or even downright weird on longer ones. By the time your reader gets to the end of a 2,000-word article—after turning page after page and reading an ad or two—odds are he or she won't remember your lead anyhow.

So finish your article on the best note you can think of, whether that ties back to your lead or not. In some cases you may even want to refer back to something that occurred midway through your piece.

For as Shakespeare once said, "All's well that ends well." Or was that Mark Twain?

7 A SHORT GUIDE TO WRITING SHORT ITEMS

Most of this book will urge you to think big when it comes to magazine writing. This chapter, however, is an exception. It's all about thinking small.

There's a good reason for thinking small, too. The market for small items is, well, huge. A magazine that runs six or seven feature-length pieces each month may run dozens of short ones. Why so much short stuff? Some magazine editors say the trend started with *USA Today* and its colorful, quick-hit approach to the news; others think that old devil television has basically destroyed people's attention spans. Whatever the reason, today's magazine readers often don't have the time or patience to dig through gobs of prose looking for the facts they need. They buy magazines to simplify their lives, not to further complicate them.

In fact, simplifying things has been the role of magazines for as long as there have been magazines. When a French publisher introduced what many historians consider the first real magazine back in 1665, he wrote that it was for "those who are either too busy or too lazy to read whole books." Two of the most successful magazines in U.S. history, *Reader's Digest* and *Time*, were founded in the early 1920s for Jazz Agers too busy to read piles of magazines and newspapers.

Luckily, writing small items can be the easiest way to break into some magazines, especially those that might never give an unfamiliar writer a shot at a longer piece. An editor who assigns you a short piece isn't taking much of a risk. If the piece falls through, the magazine won't be out much money, and it won't have a gaping hole to fill, as it would in the case of a major article gone wrong.

Other editors, though, prefer to assign small items to staff members or to regular contributors, usually just for the sake of convenience. At those magazines, small items may be the hardest sell of all.

Here are three ways to tell how receptive any given magazine may be to ideas for short items:

Check *Writer's Market*. Often magazines will specify in their listings that short items are the way to break in.

Read the magazine's guidelines for writers. They frequently say whether the magazine's small-item departments are staff-written or fair game for freelancers. In some instances, the guidelines will tell you that certain departments are the turf of one or more regular contributors, while others welcome newcomers.

Read the magazine itself. You can usually tell pretty quickly whether the small-item departments are locked up or open to all comers. Check the bylines on the items against the names on the magazine's masthead.

HOW SMALL IS SMALL?

Many magazines run items as short as 50 to 100 words. But in most cases, they'll usually assign a longer word count to give the editors enough material to work with. So plan on writing 100 to 500 words in most cases, with 200 to 250 words (one double-spaced typewritten page) being about average.

WHAT TO WRITE ABOUT

A small item can be about anything the magazine covers. But by its nature, it has to be much more tightly focused. Let's say you want to write about people who collect rock 'n' roll memorabilia. For a 2,000-word piece on the subject, you might try to interview five leading collectors across the U.S. For a 200-word item, you'd probably have room for just one subject, maybe the leading collector of Jimi Hendrix things. Or you might focus even more narrowly, say, on a major collector of guitar picks.

Your best bet in selling small items is to bring the magazine something or someone its editors didn't already know about. For example, is there anything going on in your town that might be of interest? Is someone at the local university doing research that would be relevant to what the magazine covers? Did you learn something new in reporting your most recent full-length feature for another magazine that might stand on its own as a small item?

As varied as any magazine's small items may be, there's often a common denominator: news. Your query should stress what's new about your idea: a new way to do something, a new place to visit, a new product or a new danger. If you can come up with something both new and relevant to the magazine's readers, editors will often take a chance on you even if they are uncertain of your writing skills. If you can at least deliver the reporting, they figure, someone on the magazine can fix up the writing—rewriting the piece from top to bottom if need be.

Bear in mind that monthly magazines have lead times of two months or more. So there's no point pitching a story about why readers should attend your town's June jalapeño festival to a monthly magazine in May. At that point, the magazine may have sent its June issue off to the printer, have just about wrapped up July and be hard at work on August. So plan ahead, way ahead.

Speaking of queries, you may rightly wonder whether it makes sense to write a 250-word query to propose a 200-word piece. I think it does. Editors like to feel they've had a hand in shaping your idea, so unless they're desperate for material, they're likely to give a query a fairer shake than an unsolicited finished piece. If you think it would be easier just to write the piece, by all means do that first; but then write a query based on the piece. You can probably pick up much of the same wording, so you won't have wasted a lot of effort. And if an editor likes your idea but makes a few suggestions, you can quickly rewrite your first draft accordingly.

WRITING TIGHT

I know a lot of writers who love to write long pieces and thrill at the prospect of turning in a 4,000- or 5,000-word draft, even if they know the magazine will whack it down to 2,000 words. For many of us, long is easy, short is hard.

Writing short items requires a sort of discipline that writing full-length ones does not. Your piece has to be logically structured to move from point A to point B without any digressions to point Q.

When you're only turning in 200 words or so, you have to make every word count.

Writing an effective short item is as much about what you leave out as what you put in. Let's consider that guitar pick collector I mentioned earlier. Suppose in the course of your interview, you learn that she's a distant relative of Annie Oakley, writes poetry and once shook hands with Vice President Hubert H. Humphrey. In a 2,000-word profile of her, you might find a way to weave all that in; after all, it does say something about her as a unique individual. In a 200-word piece about her guitar pick collection, however, you'd better stick to picks. Writing short items requires an almost ruthless concentration on the essential facts.

Some forms of magazine writing lend themselves better to short items than others do. Long reflective essays won't work, obviously. But single anecdotes, well told, sometimes can. A twenty-step how-to piece probably won't fit, but a three-step one might. A Q&A interview can work if both the interviewer and the interviewee keep it brief.

Short items need leads that get right to the point, transitions that do their job in as few words as possible and endings that neatly round off the piece without a lot of wordy recapitulation of what came before. In that way they're great to practice on while you hone your skills as a magazine writer.

WHAT THEY PAY

Not a whole lot, alas. A magazine that pays one dollar a word for full-length articles is likely to offer about that for short items, and sometimes a little less. That may sound fine, but as any experienced magazine writer can tell you, a 200-word piece may require as much work as a 2,000-word one. So don't count on making a career out of writing small items. Look on them as a way to break into some new markets—and to have some fun while you're at it.

8 HOW TO WRITE HOW-TO ARTICLES

The how-to article is a staple of magazine journalism—as essential to most magazines as, well, staples. Since colonial times, Americans have looked to magazines for practical advice on matters of the day. Today's article on how to buy a notebook computer is a direct descendant of the article your great-grandparents might have read on how to choose a plow.

However much the topics change (and some don't change much at all), the how-to format and writers who have mastered it remain in healthy demand. These were just a few of the how-to articles in the magazine racks when I last looked:

"How to Find the Right Doctor" (*Ladies' Home Journal*)
"How to Find the Lowest Airfare" (*Kiplinger's Personal Finance Magazine*)
"How to Get Pregnant" (*Redbook*)
"How to Answer Kids' 10 Trickiest Questions" (*Parenting*)
"How to Roast a Moist Turkey" (*Fine Cooking*)
And my favorite: "How to Marry a Rich Girl" (*Maxim*)

But common as it is, how-to writing can be surprisingly difficult for some freelancers, even experienced ones. After editing hundreds of how-to pieces (ranging from how to dress to how to invest) and writing dozens more, I've come to the conclusion that the problem is almost always one of organization. More than any other type of article, the how-to needs to be carefully crafted to give readers the information they need in exactly the order they need it.

To see how some successful how-to writers structure their pieces, I sat down and "reverse outlined" articles from a thick stack of magazines. The process of reverse outlining is explained later in this chapter. Here's what I learned by doing it:

IN THE BEGINNING

The lead of a good how-to story isn't all that different from any other type of magazine article. Its job is to get the reader to stop flipping pages and start reading. The lead sells the reader on reading that piece.

How hard the sell needs to be depends on the topic. A piece on how to improve your sex life probably doesn't require much selling. It might begin with a lively anecdote or with some news—for example, sex researchers have made a startling discovery.

But suppose your assignment is a piece on how to build a bat house for the backyard. Here, your first job would be to convince your readers that they want to have bats hanging around their property. So you might, for example, tell them that one hungry bat can put away several hundred mosquitos in an hour.

Among the most common leads for how-to pieces, I found, are three basic types:

The why-to. The bat house lead is an example of a "why-to." It tells readers *why* they should do what you're going to tell them *how* to do. A *Horticulture* piece on growing rhubarb provided another example. Not only is rhubarb tasty in sauces and pies, the lead explained, but it is also one of the most handsome food plants you can grow in an ornamental garden.

The anecdote. Another popular way to begin a how-to piece is with a little story about someone who did what you're about to discuss. A piece in *House Beautiful* on how to sell a home more quickly began with the tale of a man who made a long-unsold house more inviting simply by clearing off the kitchen counters, draping the tables with antique quilts and laying an old tweed jacket on the bed. The house sold within two weeks.

Often, the anecdote can come out of the writer's personal experience. A *Woman's Day* piece on how to hold a yard sale began with the writer's experience of making $660 at her most recent sale. A *Parents* magazine article on teaching children to share led off with the writer's not entirely successful attempt with her own three-year-old.

The news. News may be a discovery by a scientist, a pronounce-ment by a politician or simply something that will come as news to your reader. A news lead tells the reader, right at the start, that there's something to be learned here. For example, a *Runner's World* piece on lower-leg exercises got off on the right foot with a reference to "exciting new research" being done at a laboratory in California. A one-pager in *Better Homes and Gardens* on choosing a dog delivered the news that dalmatians may look great in a Disney movie, but a real one needs some serious obedience training.

IN THE MIDDLE

After the lead comes the guts of a how-to article, the part where you deliver on your promise to explain how to do something. There are probably as many ways to do that as there are things to explain, but these formats are among the most popular:

Step by step. The grandmother of all how-to formats, a step-by-step article guides readers through each stage of a process. The steps may be numbered or simply follow one another in some logical order. The *Woman's Day* yard-sale piece, for example, told readers first how to plan for a sale, then how to set up on the day of the sale, and finally what to do during the sale.

An *Inc.* article on how to get start-up funding for a small business took another approach. It followed one successful entrepreneur, step by step, through the process.

A more lighthearted piece in *Self* on "How to Get Over Party Phobia," offered "10 easy steps from wall flower to belle of the ball." For example: "3. Look around; some guests are even more uncomfortable than you are."

The challenge in the step-by-step article is how to cover all the steps without belaboring the obvious. The trick is often to make the obvious seem less so. For example, in an article on painting a gazebo, you probably wouldn't want to begin with, "1. Open the can of paint." But you might get away with something like: "1. Don't forget to give the can of paint a couple of vigorous shakes before you open it."

Roundup. Sometimes, a topic doesn't lend itself to step-by-step treatment. Perhaps there are many different ways to do something but

51

the steps themselves are self-evident. That's when a roundup works better. Roundups often have a number in the headline: "47 Simple Ways to Whatever." The piece itself may use numbers or "bullets" (those big black dots or squares at the beginning of a paragraph) to separate items. *Redbook*, for example, ran a travel piece on "33 Ways to Save Money on Your Next Vacation." *Men's Health* offered its readers thirty-three ways to get more control over their time. Must be something magical about that number thirty-three. . . .

Expository. That's what I call this format for lack of a less pompous word. Some how-to stories won't work in either a step-by-step or a roundup format. Often that's because the topic is so broad or readers' needs so varied that no one set of advice will fit everybody. Such articles are often written in a more traditional expository style that allows the writer to move from idea to idea as gracefully as possible. In a cover story on "How to Get Ahead in America," *Fortune* magazine looked at how Americans of different ages and in different fields were coping with change in the workplace. A step-by-step format ("Step 1: Compliment your boss on his taste in ties . . .") wouldn't have done the job as effectively.

Whatever format you choose for your how-to piece, your goal, notes veteran how-to writer Tom Philbin, is to "anticipate the reader's informational needs and not leave any questions in his or her mind." So before you do any reporting, you may find it useful to jot down what you'd want to know if you were the reader of such a piece. If you're already an expert on your topic, a good reality check is to ask a nonexpert from among your friends what his or her questions would be.

AND IN THE END

How-to articles tend to wind up quickly. If your piece is a roundup, you may just want to finish on the last item, with no final flourishes at all. (Make sure that item doesn't end with a dull thud, though.)

Or, you may want to try one of these approaches:

A final anecdote. Just as a colorful anecdote can be a wise way to begin a how-to article, it can also be a nice note to end on. The *Inc.* piece on one entrepreneur's quest for start-up capital ended with him getting a line of credit. The *House Beautiful* piece on fixing up a home for quick sale finished with a few final words of wisdom from the man

How to Outline in Reverse

Reverse outlining is an idea I borrowed from the world of manufacturing, one that can be useful in learning how to write all kinds of magazine articles. In a process called "reverse engineering," a manufacturer will buy a competitor's product, take it apart and see what can be learned from its design and construction. Some people might call that thievery, but who are we to judge?

Reverse outlining is the journalistic equivalent. It means taking a published piece and making an outline of its structure, much like the author of that article might have done before writing it. Reverse outlining is not only a good way to learn how certain types of articles are constructed but also to see how a particular magazine likes to approach a topic. You will almost certainly learn something about how an article was put together that wasn't immediately obvious when you first read it.

A reverse outline can be as simple or as detailed as you want. Nobody will grade you on it. You don't even have to use Roman numerals unless you really want to.

I stumbled on reverse outlining all by myself, but I strongly doubt I invented the idea. In fact, reverse outlining by one name or another probably has a long and glorious history. The novelist and, yes, magazine writer F. Scott Fitzgerald, for example, may have been an early practitioner. When he went to work in Hollywood in the 1930s, he taught himself the craft of screenwriting by watching movies and outlining their plots on note cards.

who'd helped sell the house described in the story's lead.

A call to action. An alternative approach is to tell your readers that they're now ready to act on what they've just learned. A piece in *Good Housekeeping* on how to write personal notes ended by urging the reader to put pen to paper that very day.

Summing up. An unusually long or complex how-to article may require a final paragraph or two to pull together the article's most important lessons. The *Fortune* piece on getting ahead in America closed with the thought that "the only real security is the ability to grow, change and adapt." That seems like good advice for *Fortune*'s readers—and for magazine writers, as well.

9 WRITING ABOUT PEOPLE, FAMOUS AND OTHERWISE

There's no truer truism in journalism than this: People like to read about people. Not for nothing is *People Magazine* the most profitable title in the U.S.

Who makes a good subject for a personality profile? Just about anyone who has an interesting story to tell. (Interesting enough, that is, to get an editor to assign it.) Your subject needn't be a celebrity, though that never hurts. Readers already have at least some curiosity about famous people, whereas with unknown people, you have to stir their curiosity through your writing. It's just a lot easier to get readers interested in a movie star than, say, a mail carrier— even if the mail carrier is a far more fascinating person.

People who aren't yet celebrated often make the most memorable profiles. Joseph Mitchell, a writer for *The New Yorker* and a master of the form, wrote about a Manhattan street preacher, a nine-year-old genius and the woman in a ticket cage outside a seedy movie theater—plus any number of other people whose unusual lives and peculiar ways of making a living defy easy description.

We'll look briefly at profiling ordinary people, then at celebrity journalism.

JUST FOLKS
Ask yourself: Who is the most fascinating person in your town? Maybe it's a soccer coach, a children's book author, a Korean War hero or an undertaker who's also a competitive ballroom dancing champion. Behind most fascinating people is a fascinating tale of how they got that way.

Your advantage in profiling local people is just that—they're local. You may be the only writer who has ever seen a possible story in them or brought them to the attention of some faraway editor.

The disadvantage, of course, is that they may be harder to sell to a magazine editor than someone who is already nationally known and may have been written about dozens of times. Unless the soccer coach has a truly inspiring tale to tell, chances are magazines like *Life* or *Reader's Digest* won't be interested. They probably get pitched on coach stories every other day. But a magazine on coaching might be interested. Or a magazine on soccer. Or the nearest city or regional magazine. Or, if no magazine bites, a nearby newspaper. As with any kind of story, your query should explain as clearly as possible why a story about that person belongs in that publication and why you should be the one to write it.

Timeliness helps, too. Let's say your town is home to one of the nation's foremost beekeepers. He's been keeping bees since childhood, has won every important beekeeping award and wrote the definitive book on the subject. He is truly King of the Bees. Interesting enough so far, but one fundamental question remains unanswered: Why should a magazine run a piece about this guy now? In the jargon of journalism, what's your "news peg"?

Here are some possible news pegs for your beekeeper story, ranging from the weakest to the strongest:

1. May has been proclaimed National Bee Appreciation month.
2. U.S. honey production has recently doubled, thanks to important advances in beekeeping technology.
3. The fiftieth anniversary edition of the beekeeper's book.
4. The President has taken up beekeeping as a hobby.
5. Madonna is abandoning music to devote her life to bees.
6. Madonna has been seen in the company of your local beekeeper.
7. Killer bees have been sighted off both coasts of the United States, and only your beekeeper knows how to stop them.

INTERVIEWING ORDINARY PEOPLE

Celebrities know the game. They know how to give you colorful quotes, even if their press agents put those quotes in their mouths.

Ordinary people, however, are more prone to giving colorless, yes or I-don't-know answers. They may be shy when it comes to talking about themselves, or they may just not think their lives are as interesting as you do. So be prepared to take the time to win your subject's trust, and stand ready to go back again and again until you've got all the details you need to sit down and write.

But be careful. Libel laws are tougher on stories about everyday people than they are on stories about celebrities. And for good reason. People who aren't accustomed to dealing with the media often don't realize, until it's too late, what their words are going to look like in print. Excited by the prospect of having their names and maybe even their pictures in a magazine, they may tell you things that, if published, would cause them or others great embarrassment.

So your job as a profile writer is tricky. You owe your readers a story that's true and interesting. You also have an obligation to your subjects. You're not obliged to twist the truth to make them look better or to leave out essential facts that your subjects would rather the world not know. But you do owe them a story that's fair, doesn't go for cheap laughs at their expense and doesn't invade every last corner of their privacy—unless there's a good reason for it.

Since ordinary people don't know the rules, the person you're writing about may ask to see a copy of your story before you send it to the magazine. Giving in is almost always a bad idea. Your subject may demand any number of changes or even say that he or she doesn't want to be written about, period.

Most writers I know tell their subjects that the magazine's policy is not to show manuscripts to anyone before publication (whether it has such a policy or not). If the magazine you're writing for has fact checkers, as most magazines do, you can tell your subject that they will be in touch to verify the information in the article.

If the magazine doesn't have fact checkers, you may want to do it yourself. (This is in addition to all the other efforts you will have made to this point to check and recheck your facts.) Go through the facts in your article with your subject, preferably by telephone. Don't read anything verbatim, or the subject may try to change your wording; just lay out the facts and ask if they are correct. Never, never read a direct quote back to a subject; paraphrase it instead. Otherwise, your subject may take a perfectly fine, conversational

56

quote and try to turn it into something more grammatically elegant—and ultimately more boring. Your goal, as an editor I knew used to say, should be "fact checking, not fact wrecking."

CELEBRITY JOURNALISM
There's an oxymoron for you. With each passing year, celebrity journalism seems to be less about journalism and more about celebrity. The fad as I write this (hopefully to pass by the time you read this) is for major magazines to turn their pages over to movie stars interviewing themselves. No, I don't mean movie stars interviewing other movie stars: I mean Sharon Stone interviewing Sharon Stone. (Call me old-fashioned, but in my day, sonny, you didn't have journalism unless a journalist was involved somewhere in the process.)

Whatever strange forms celebrity journalism may take in the future, it's almost a given that magazines will need celebrity profiles and lots of them. And in case you aren't interested in movie stars, bear in mind that a celebrity can be almost anyone whose name is known to the general public. It might be a best-selling author, an astronaut, a business tycoon, a mass murderer or the person who finds a cure for the common cold. Magazine editors know that readers are interested in famous people—in the paths they took to become famous, in their off-stage lives (whether inspiring or sordid) and their private personas (whether gracious or monstrous). Individual celebrities may come and go, but the public's hunger for knowing more about the celebrity du jour never seems to waver.

BREAKING IN
How do you cash in on this national obsession with celebrities? Unlike any other kind of magazine writing I can think of, celebrity profiles rarely start with a story idea. Instead, they begin with access. That is, what celebrated person can you get in to see? Once you know that, you can begin to think of an angle for your story and about the kinds of magazines that might be interested in buying it.

If your uncle is the head of a major television network, access may not be a problem for you. And if you regularly write for magazines but haven't done any celebrity profiles, an editor who is familiar with your other work may be happy to give you a shot at one.

But if you're a beginner without any special connections, you'll have to be resourceful. Once again, there's a lot to be said for starting locally. Does someone famous live in your town? Did a celebrity grow up there and still return now and then? Did your mother go to high school with a future celeb or the parent of one? Is some local celebrity (the newspaper cartoonist or radio host, for instance) beginning to catch on nationally?

Now, here's the tricky part. If you ask a celebrated person (or one's publicist) for an interview, the first question is likely to be: "Who are you writing for?" If you can't name a magazine, you're going to come off like an amateur, a stalker or both. At the same time, you have to be careful not to query a magazine with an idea for a celebrity piece you don't have a hope of delivering.

This is one of those chicken-or-egg dilemmas for which there is no correct answer. My advice would be to approach the magazine first, saying you'd like to write about the celebrated So-and-So, and you believe you can get an interview through your local connections. The magazine may say no, of course, in which case you won't have bothered the celebrity needlessly. If the magazine says yes, but the celebrity says no, there's no harm done either, since you didn't promise the magazine you could absolutely get the interview. And if both the magazine and the celebrity say yes, you're in business.

ARRANGING INTERVIEWS

Most celebrities these days have publicists. Even some publicists seem to have publicists.

The publicist may work directly for the celebrity or for the celebrity's TV network, publishing house or whatever. Though you might think the job of a publicist is to get publicity, sometimes it's just the opposite. Publicists spend a lot of their time fending off writers who want to interview their clients. Publicists are the gatekeepers to the rich and famous, and they can make your life as an interviewer a pleasure or a penance.

So to approach any given celebrity, you'll usually have to track down that person's publicist. Want to interview a famous author? Find out which publisher brought out his or her most recent book and call the PR department. A famed quarterback? Call the team's press office. A celebrated scientist? Try his or her university.

Be prepared to explain the basic angle of your story, but don't feel obligated to offer every last detail. Have an idea of how much time you need (ask for at least an hour; less time is rarely enough, and once you get in the door and firmly planted in a chair you can often get more). Keep your editor's phone number at hand in case the publicist wants to verify that you have a real assignment. And be prepared for the possibility of rejection.

However much they craved publicity on the way up or will crave it again on the way down, celebrities at the pinnacles of their careers know that magazines need them more than they need magazines. Your best shot at getting to an otherwise elusive celebrity is when he or she has something to sell: a new movie, a new perfume, a new explanation for being caught in a hot tub with a thirteen-year-old. Try to strike when the time is right. If you want to interview authors, for example, watch out for news of forthcoming books.

CELEBRITIES AND THEIR DEMANDS

Once upon a time, celebrities were happy just to appear on magazine covers; now some of them want to choose the photo and control everything else about the article—even, in some cases, who writes it. So any publicist you approach may have a list of demands to be agreed to before the celebrity will talk. That could include approving the questions you ask, the quotes you ultimately use and who knows what all else.

Don't agree to anything, but put the publicist in touch with your editor. Let them work it out.

PREPARING FOR THE INTERVIEW

Celebrity journalism is easy in one respect. There is so much written about famous people that you rarely have to start your research from scratch. Of course, you can't trust everything you read, even if you've seen the same "fact" or "quote" over and over again. Anecdotes about celebrities tend to take on lives of their own and to be repeated unchallenged in successive stories. Sometimes, celebrity profiles are simply "written from the clips"—in other words, assembled entirely from previously published materials, usually because the celebrity was uncooperative.

59

So, as you plow through the material you've assembled, be skeptical and selective. Consider the source: Some magazines and newspapers are obviously more scrupulous than others in sticking to the facts (though they may still get things wrong). One book about your subject may be too vicious, another may be far too laudatory. If you research your subject on-line, you're apt to find just about anything, from the factual to the far-fetched.

INTERVIEWING CELEBRITIES

First, find out how much time you've got. If the interview is only for a half hour, you'll need to choose your questions more carefully.

The publicist may want to sit in on your interview. Ideally, he or she will stay quietly off to the side rather than try to answer questions for the celebrity or ask questions for you.

Use a tape recorder unless the celebrity objects. Take notes of key points. If your tape recorder goes kaput, you may have to write from your notes alone.

Don't waste time asking questions like "Is it true you were born in Omaha, Nebraska?" or "What year did your first book come out?" Those questions are easily answered from reference materials, and celebrities tend to get cranky when they have to field them for the umpteenth time.

To give your piece some color (and to prove to your readers that you were actually there), look around. If you're in the celebrity's office, write down how it's decorated, what kinds of pictures hang on the walls, what sort of stuff clutters the desk. Note how your subject looks. What is he wearing? Is she relaxed or fidgety? Is he pale or tanned? Is she smoking and, if so, what?

When I interviewed Muppet creator Jim Henson some years ago, I was struck by how quiet and laid-back he seemed—until that is, he stuck his hand into a Kermit the Frog puppet and suddenly burst to life. By paying as much attention to how Henson was acting as to what he was saying, I was able to give a fuller picture of the man.

Save your toughest questions for last, or at least for late in the interview; you don't want to get booted out the door before you've at least got some material to work with. When I profiled television interviewer Ted Koppel, I couldn't avoid asking him about his haircut, which was, at the time, inspiring some nasty comparisons to

Howdy Doody and *MAD Magazine*'s Alfred E. Neuman. So once I'd been through all my more polite questions, I asked Koppel that one. Fortunately, he handled it gracefully, proving that he could not only dish out tough questions but take one occasionally, too.

Plan to interview other people who know the celebrity to round out your portrait. The celebrity or publicist can give you a list and sometimes make it easier for you to contact them. Don't expect anyone on the list to be especially critical of your subject, of course. If you want a more outspoken opinion, look for leads in other stories you've read for your research.

Finally, confirm your interview a day or two in advance. I learned this lesson when I flew to Florida to interview Arnold Palmer. Though the interview had been arranged weeks earlier through the great golfer's representatives, apparently nobody had told him. So when I showed up in his office, he didn't have the faintest idea who I was or what I was there for. Fortunately, Arnold Palmer is among the most decent celebrities around; he stopped what he was doing, leaned back in his chair and gave me a long interview. Not everybody would have.

WRITING THE PIECE

If you want to write a good celebrity profile, write it for your readers. If you want to write a bad one, write it for the celebrity.

However nice a famous person may be to you, he or she is not your friend and never will be. Your job is not to flatter your subject or put him or her on an even higher pedestal. Your job is to tell the truth—seriously, humorously or however the magazine expects.

If beginners make one common mistake, it is in trying to be so nice that even their famous subjects wouldn't recognize themselves. The best profiles aim to render their subjects "warts and all," as the old saying goes. A more modern—and somewhat grosser—expression I heard some years ago is "nose picker." A nose picker is an unflattering detail about your subject, preferably fairly high up in the piece. By showing your subject picking her nose, losing his temper or whatever, you clue the reader that you're writing about a real human being, not a paragon. And readers are more interested in people than paragons, anyway.

61

10 INTERVIEWS THAT GET PEOPLE TALKING

Interviews are an important part of many magazine articles. In some cases, they *are* the article.

Indeed, the interview article or Q&A is one of the most versatile forms of journalism—a mainstay of publications as diverse as *Playboy* and *The Paris Review*, *Rolling Stone* and *Reader's Digest*. But as writers frequently discover when they take their first shot at one, interviews are not as easy as they look. Though the best of them read much like real conversations, they are often the result of painstaking cutting and rearranging. Here, in question-and-answer form, are some answers to the most common questions about interviews:

Q. Most interviews begin with a short introduction. What's its role?
A. To give some background on the person being interviewed and perhaps on the circumstances of the interview, such as where and when it took place. Ideally, the introduction will also stress a news angle: Why should this person be of interest to the reader at this time?

Q. How should the interview begin?
A. In talking about interviews, you have to make a distinction between the actual interview that takes place between a reporter and a subject and the interview as it will eventually appear in print. The actual interview should usually begin with some soft questions to set the subject at ease and get him or her warmed up for more difficult questions later on. The printed interview, however, should begin with something fairly provocative. Like any other form of journalism, an interview has to hook readers right from the start.

Q. What if the early answers in the actual interview aren't very interesting?
A. Put them later or discard them altogether.

Q. Then it's OK to rearrange the interview?
A. Most publications have no quarrel with that. The point of an interview piece isn't to make a stenographic record of your conversation, but to present what the interviewee has to say as clearly and engagingly as possible. And that often means rearranging things a bit.

Q. Are there any exceptions?
A. Probably. If, for example, your interview subject has been charged with a crime or is running for political office—or both— you might want to use the interview verbatim. In those instances, every word could be critical.

Q. How about altering quotes?
A. You don't want to put words in a subject's mouth, but you'll do both subject and reader a favor if you take some words out. "Um," for example. Or, "Excuse me, I have to let the dog in." You may also want to fix grammatical lapses and cut needless repetition.

Q. Any other advice on quotes?
A. Don't let them drag on forever, or you'll risk losing the reader. If your interviewee has a long (but good) story to tell, see if there's a way to break it up in your manuscript by interjecting a short question or two.

Q. Such as?
A. Yes, "Such as?" can work. Or something like, "Then what happened?"

Q. How about changing your questions in the printed interview?
A. It's fine to sharpen your questions so they lead more smoothly into the answers that follow. Obviously, though, you don't want to change the question so much that it then distorts the meaning of the answer.

Q. What if the interviewee wants to see the manuscript before it's printed?
A. How you handle that depends on the policy of your publication and on any agreement you made with the subject prior to the inter-

view. Some publications allow interview subjects the courtesy of reviewing the piece—on the clear understanding that they want to make sure it's factually accurate—not that they're giving up editorial control over it.

Q. Isn't there a danger in that?
A. Sure. On rare occasions, the subject may be horrified by what he or she said earlier and try to back out of the whole project. More commonly, subjects will want to reword their answers into what they think of as more "correct" (in other words, stilted) English. This happens most often with people who are unaccustomed to being interviewed. One way around that problem is to read them a paraphrase of their answers; they'll be able to verify that they said such-and-such, but they won't be tempted to dress up the way they said it.

Q. What do you do if the subject wants to make changes?
A. If it's something minor or a change that will actually improve the piece, go ahead. On major changes, however, you should probably talk it over with your editor.

Q. What kinds of people make the best interview subjects?
A. People with ideas—authors, scientists, business leaders. They must have something interesting to say, and they must be able to say it in language your readers will understand.

Q. How should the interviewer prepare?
A. By reading everything by and about your subject that you can get your hands on. Sometimes it's also useful to talk to people who know him or her and get their insights. It's almost impossible to overprepare. Besides, your subject will be flattered that you went to all that trouble.

Q. Should you write out your questions?
A. Yes, and in a logical order where one thing leads to another. Be flexible, though. During the course of the interview, other questions are bound to occur to you, or your subject may take the conversation off into unexpected territory.

Q. Should you submit your questions to your subject in advance?
A. No, unless that's the only way to get the interview, and your editor has agreed for you to do it. However, it's often useful to give

64

subjects a general idea of the areas you want to discuss when you first call to set up the interview. That allows them some time to focus their thoughts.

Q. What equipment do you need?
A. A portable tape recorder with strong batteries. Pocket-size microcassette recorders with built-in microphones are ideal. Another useful piece of equipment is a transcribing machine with a foot pedal, especially if you plan to do interviews fairly often.

Q. What about bringing a camera along?
A. If you're on assignment for a small publication that doesn't have the budget to send a photographer, you might try taking some photos yourself. But you should probably do it after the interview is safely on tape and before your subject runs out of patience. If your publication is planning to send a photographer, try to schedule your interview for a time when the photographer won't be there. Otherwise, the two of you will be competing for the subject's attention and tripping all over each other.

Q. Should you transcribe the tape yourself or have a professional transcriber do it?
A. Do it yourself if you have time. It's one of the most boring jobs in magazine writing, but you'll often pick up nuances you'd miss in a transcript. Also, you may learn ways to improve your interviewing technique by reliving the experience.

Q. Once you've finished the transcript, what do you do?
A. Go through it and highlight the best material. Then make a brief outline of how the pieces will fit together.

Q. What if you start to write a Q&A and discover gaps—such as a question you should have asked, but didn't?
A. Often you can go back to your subject with a few follow-up questions. Unless subjects are terribly busy or self-important, they'll usually make themselves available. It's in their interest as much as yours that the published interview turn out well.

Q. Is it better to interview in person or by phone?
A. In-person interviews tend to work out best, as long as you have the time to go and your publication has the money to send you.

You'll soak up more atmosphere and come up with some good questions based on what you see. It's possible to do a good interview by phone, though. In fact, many subjects are actually more comfortable that way. Talking into the phone is more natural to most of us than talking into a tape recorder.

Q. How much interview time should you ask for?
A. At least forty-five minutes to an hour. Some Q&As are the result of many hours of interviewing spread over several sessions. *Playboy* instructed its interviewers to spend as much time with an interview subject as he or she would allow—and then ask for more.

Q. What's the best way to end the interview?
A. The printed interview (as opposed to the actual one) should end the same way it began—on a lively, provocative note. When all else fails, end on a question that asks your subject to look forward. For example, what are his or her future plans?

Q. And what's the best way to end the actual interview?
A. One often fruitful way is to ask your subject if there's anything he or she would care to add. That frequently opens up an avenue of discussion you wouldn't otherwise have known about.

Q. Anything to add?
A. No, but thanks for asking.

11 WRITING FROM YOUR PERSONAL EXPERIENCE

Most of the pieces you write for magazines will concern other people, places and things. Sometimes, though, you'll have a chance to write about a subject that's a little closer to home: yourself.

In this chapter we'll look at some of the opportunities magazines provide for first-person writing. As you read along, remember that unlike most of the other kinds of writing explored in this book, the success of first-person writing depends to a huge extent on the personality you bring to your prose. A writer whose voice is distinctive and fascinating in its own right can sometimes make the most mundane subject come alive on the page. A writer who hasn't yet developed a distinctive style could be hard-pressed to make even an interesting subject seem, uh, interesting.

Think for a second of the writers whose first-person pieces you might see on a major magazine's table of contents. Would you automatically turn to a piece if the byline happened to be Dave Barry? Or John Updike? Or Joan Didion? Now, suppose the subject of Barry's, Updike's or Didion's piece was doing the laundry.... Would you still read it? Probably so, if only to see how a deft writer can make something out of such a familiar subject.

That's not to say that you have to be a famous writer to sell a first-person piece. In some cases, it undoubtedly helps. But at many magazines, the uniqueness of your voice and the power of the story you have to tell are far more important. You may find first-person pieces easier to market than many other types, especially when you're just starting out. Lots of writers can do a routine how-to piece or a personality profile. But only you are living your life, with its own set of experiences, past and present. In the words of the great purple dinosaur Barney, "You are special."

WRITING THE PERSONAL ESSAY

The word *essay* is a cousin of the word *assay*, which means to examine something (like a chunk of rock) to determine whether it contains anything valuable (such as gold). There's a practical point to this little etymology lesson: Magazine editors don't want your rocks. What they're interested in is the gold those rocks contain.

A story about some experience you've had may be the raw material (in other words, the rock) for an essay, but it's rarely an essay (the gold) in and of itself. Many other people—in fact, many other writers—may have had a similar experience. What makes yours special is the insight you bring to it. Albert DiBartolomeo, a writer and writing teacher whose powerful essays appear in such publications as *Philadelphia Magazine* and *Reader's Digest*, says a personal essay isn't just about an experience but "experience plus reflection."

So, ask yourself: What experiences have you had that gave you some special insight into life? If you're like many writers, you may not know exactly what that insight was until you begin to get some words down on paper. That's where some of the best reflection always seems to happen. If your experience is one that many magazine readers have shared, all the better. Whatever you felt, they may feel too—even though they were unaware they felt that way until you showed them.

Some magazine writers will never do a personal essay and others may do one or two, figuring that's all they have to say. But a few writers manage to assay the rocks of their personal experience repeatedly, finding gold again and again.

Paula Spencer sells more than a dozen essays a year to such magazines as *Glamour*, *Parenting* and *Woman's Day*. One of her secrets is keeping a journal, as she has done for more than thirty years. "My journal is very different from what appears on the written essay page," she says, "but it does get me in an introspective mode. I'm also very opinionated—and that helps a lot."

PUTTING YOURSELF IN THE STORY

Not every experience you have in life will lead to an essay or, for that matter, be worth a whole lot of reflection. Sometimes, though, you can use such material in other types of pieces. You won't strike gold in every rock you assay, but you may find some silver or copper or iron.

Let's say you recently had your kitchen remodeled, and the contractor you hired proved to be a lunatic. He missed his first three appointments, causing you untold aggravation, and when he finally did show up, he hung half your cabinets upside down. You might not want to write an entire essay about the experience, but you could possibly use it as the lead for a query and (if you get the assignment) as an anecdote in a piece on hiring a good contractor.

Personal experiences can enrich your magazine articles in many other ways. Years ago, the tradition in journalism was for reporters to stay totally out of the story if at all possible. Even if someone you were trying to interview happened to slug you, you were expected to say, "so-and-so suddenly lunged forward and hit a reporter on the nose," rather than come right out and admit it was your nose. Times change, and today many writers don't hesitate to include a bit of themselves in articles that aren't basically about them.

Travel writing is one area where first- and third-person writing often mingle. A piece on New Orleans might include all the usual tourist spots but also describe the little side street cafe where you, writing in the first person, found the best cup of coffee you've ever had. An article on white-water rafting on the Colorado River may be much more vivid if you break in from time to time to share how elated (or terrified) you felt when your raft started spinning out of control.

The trick here is to strike the right balance. Sometimes a little glimpse of the writer is enough to spice up what would otherwise be a fairly routine piece, while any more than that could seem obtrusive, vain or downright obnoxious. Other times, a piece is more powerful if it focuses largely on the writer's reaction to a place or an experience rather than on the place or experience itself. When in doubt, consult with your editor about how much of yourself you can safely inject into your article. Editors often have strong opinions in these matters, and magazines have their own customary approaches. Delivering something different from what the editor envisioned can result in an experience far more terrifying than anything the Colorado River could possibly dish up.

One additional caution: As a creative writer you may be tempted to invent things now and then, either to improve on what really happened or to concoct episodes that never occurred in the first place. If you're writing a book, you can probably get away with it, since books are not held to the same rigorous standards of fact checking as magazines. So if you want to write about an imaginary affair with Elvis Presley, do it as a book. Because if you do it as a magazine article, you'd better have the motel receipts.

SOME SOOTHING WORDS ABOUT REJECTION

Rejection is so much a part of the magazine writer's life that there's a whole chapter on the subject later in this book. But rejection can sting especially hard when the piece that's being turned down is about you. Does rejection mean that your experiences weren't important enough? Or that your insights weren't, well, insightful enough?

To be honest, sometimes it does. We all have experiences or thoughts that seem significant to us but ho-hum to all but our most devoted friends and relatives. Many times, though, it has nothing to do with you, but rather with a particular magazine's needs. The phrase "doesn't meet our needs at this time," found on many magazines' rejection slips, sometimes really means what it says. For example, a perfectly fine personal essay may be rejected if the magazine recently covered the subject or if it already has a similar piece in its inventory for future use.

Occasionally, timing works in the writer's favor. As a magazine editor, I once bought a college professor's essay about taking tae kwon do classes, in large part because it arrived just as we were preparing a major article on the subject. The essay was terrific in its own right, but it wasn't the kind of piece we normally ran. Had we not been doing the other piece (to which we attached the professor's essay as a sidebar), I would never have bought it. And had it come in six months earlier or two months later, I wouldn't have had any use for it either.

So never discount the role of luck in placing your essays. Just hope for more of the good kind than that other kind. And keep digging those rocks.

SELLING YOUR ESSAYS

As usual, you'll save yourself a lot of wasted effort if you really study the magazines you want to write personal essays for. Does the magazine run first-person pieces at all? Are they always by famous writers or sometimes by not-yet-famous ones? Does it use only regular columnists, or is it open to anybody? Are its pieces funny or serious or both? If it's a magazine for parents, does it run essays by mothers? By fathers? How about grandparents?

You'll also get a sense of the length of essays the magazine prefers and their level of sophistication. An essay that's right for *The Atlantic Monthly* might be out of place in *Outlaw Biker*.

When in doubt, query. Editors often can't tell if they would buy your essay without seeing the whole piece, but they can let you know whether your idea seems appropriate—or way off the mark. And, as I mentioned back in chapter four, an editor's invitation to submit an essay may mean that it will be read more carefully and more favorably than one that showed up at the door uninvited.

Be prepared to write on spec, without any promise of money if the magazine doesn't want to buy your essay. Some magazines expect essay writers to work on spec even if the writer has already been published in that very magazine.

If you write an essay and your target magazine doesn't buy it, don't give up. Is there another magazine that might be interested in the piece—either as is or with a bit of reworking? Often it pays to have more than one market in mind even before you write an essay, especially if you're doing it on spec. If nothing else, hang onto your essays for your family. A decade or two from now, nobody may want to read your old how-to articles, but an essay in which you shared something of yourself could be a different story.

12 HOW TO BE A WHIZ AT WRITING A QUIZ

The term *quiz*, according to one popular account, was invented by a Dublin theater manager who bet he could get a new word into the English language overnight. He paid some kids to scrawl it in chalk all over his city, and by the next day *quiz* was on almost every Dubliner's lips (not to mention their walls, front doors and window boxes).

If *quiz* needed less than twenty-four hours to become part of the language, it probably didn't take much more than forty-eight to find its way into magazines. And quizzes have been part of many magazines ever since.

Today, quizzes are:
  (a) popular with magazine editors
  (b) unpopular with magazine editors
  (c) all of the above

The answer is (c). Some magazine editors swear by quizzes, while others swear at them. The quiz lovers among editors see them as an interactive exercise readers love and sometimes even learn a few things from. Here, for example, are some quizzes I spotted not long ago at the local newsstand:

"Test Your Fire Safety IQ" (*Child*)

"Are You Happy?" (*New Woman*)

"Could You Be Depressed?" (*Walking Magazine*)

"Is It Really Over?" (*Seventeen*)

"Are You a Stress Mess?" (*YM*)

"Do You Talk Too Much?" (*Prevention*)

While some magazines, like those, are obviously open to quizzes, other editors would just as soon run phone book listings—in Serbo-Croatian. They think quizzes turn off readers by reminding them too much of homework.

So if you want to create quizzes, the first rule is to see which magazines will even consider them. That means checking whether a magazine you want to write for has run quizzes in recent months and what kinds of topics those quizzes covered. If you're scanning tables of contents in the supermarket express line, look for titles with a question mark after them.

TEST YOUR QUIZ IQ

1. True or false: Make it fun.
(**True.**) You can take some of the "homework" sting off a quiz by making sure the reader gets a few laughs or learns a few amazing facts along the way. I once edited a quiz on the legal rights of investors that the writer based on some fascinating court cases he'd dug up. If a writer could make that subject interesting, you can make just about anything interesting.

2. True or false: Make it easy.
(**False.**) At least don't make it too easy. Some quizzes have no right or wrong answers but simply ask readers about their health, emotions or some other aspect of their lives. But when you're quizzing readers on their general knowledge, watch out. Readers who get all the answers right won't learn anything and may even feel you've wasted their time. At the same time, don't make it too hard. Readers who don't get any answers right are likely to feel like dopes—for bothering with your quiz if nothing else.

There are no formal rules on how tough a quiz should be, but I don't think you'll go far wrong if in, say, a ten-question quiz you give your readers five fairly easy ones, three somewhat more difficult ones and two tough (but not impossible) ones. Obviously it helps to know as much as you can about your readers and their level of sophistication about the topic. What would be an easy question in a magazine for stockbrokers might be a tough one in a magazine for novice investors. Warren Boroson, a veteran free-lancer who has done quizzes on everything from baseball to famous misquotations, says the secret of creating good, hard quiz questions is to "find something that startles you as a writer."

3. True or false: Keep it short.
(**True.**) No quiz should go on so long that readers tire of it or have to get up and sharpen their pencils two or three times. Twenty questions may be about the limit, with five to ten being even better. Many magazines that run quizzes use them as sidebars to longer articles on related topics, so you're lucky to get even half a page of space (maybe 500 words at most). For a bit more on quizzes as sidebars, see chapter thirteen.

To write a punchy quiz, try to keep your introduction brief. Usually a paragraph or two will do; sometimes the headline alone will suffice.

The questions should get right to the point, as well. If your quiz is multiple choice, keep the choices to a minimum. Often (a) and (b) are enough. If you find yourself up to (f) or (g), you're writing a college entrance exam, not a magazine quiz.

Your explanations of the correct answers will often need to run a little longer, especially if you're quoting experts with long academic titles. But still aim to be as concise as possible. Complicated "on the one hand . . . but on the other hand" kinds of answers not only take up a lot of space on the page but tend to leave readers' heads spinning. It's better for all concerned to replace any question that requires a complex answer with something a little more straightforward.

KINDS OF QUIZZES
Most quizzes follow the time-honored formats we all learned in school. While those formats may seem clichéd by now (another reason some editors despise them), they do have one clear advantage: You don't have to waste a lot of space instructing your reader on how to take the quiz. Instead, the reader can just dive in and do it.

True/false quizzes may be the most common type in magazines today. Multiple choice probably runs a close second. Some writers mix them up, giving readers a bit of true/false and a bit of multiple choice in the same quiz for the sake of variety.

You can also craft the sort of quiz that asks readers to match the entries in Column A to those in Column B. This technique seems to work best with trivia and relatively light topics rather than those that require some explanation of the answers. For example, I wrote a quiz some years ago called "Monikers Aweigh!" asking readers to match the great ocean liners (Column A) with their nicknames (Column B). Once I'd told readers which nickname belonged to which ship, there wasn't much left to do but sail off quietly into the sunset.

13 SIDEBARS THAT SELL

Sidebars are to magazine articles what Jim was to Huck, Pancho was to Cisco, Barney was to Fred. They don't get top billing, but the story wouldn't be the same without them.

It would be a stretch to say that sidebars are more important than the articles they accompany, or that a socko sidebar will sell an otherwise crummy manuscript. But a great sidebar or series of sidebars can make a well-crafted article even better. And a stellar sidebar idea will help any article proposal stand out from the pack.

The time to start thinking about sidebars is even before you write your query. First, scan a few recent issues of your target magazine to see if it uses sidebars. If it does, see if it favors sidebars of a particular length or type. We'll get into some of the common varieties in just a moment.

When you write your query, describe a few aspects of the story that you think would lend themselves to sidebar treatment. That will help the editor visualize what the finished article might look like. Even more important, it will show the editor that you have already invested some serious thought in the piece. That alone should move your query into the semifinals.

When you get a go-ahead and begin your reporting, be open to new sidebar possibilities that may pop up along the way. Once, for example, when I was well into writing a magazine article on people who collect James Bond memorabilia, I discovered that Bond's creator, Ian Fleming, was himself a passionate collector of early scientific books. The sidebar on Ian Fleming, collector, turned out to be at least as interesting as the story I'd set out to do.

There's no better guide to sidebars that will sell than sidebars that actually have sold. So a while back, I sat down with more than one hundred magazines. Here, in roughly descending order of prominence, are the kinds of sidebars you're most likely to see— and to sell.

THE USEFUL LIST SIDEBAR

The Useful List may be the most common variety of sidebar in magazines today, for a couple of obvious reasons. For one thing, people like lists. We enjoy making lists (grocery lists, to-do lists, enemies lists), and we enjoy reading them (best-dressed lists, best-seller lists, ex-Presidents' enemies lists).

From a magazine editor's point of view, the list format has another advantage: It's a remarkably compact way of delivering information. By simply listing items, either by number or after those big black dots that typographers call "bullets," a magazine doesn't need a lot of wordy transitions to get from idea to idea.

Some lists elaborate on points made in the main article. *Horticulture*, for example, accompanied an article on winter gardening on the West Coast with a list of vegetables the author had found particularly hardy. *McCall's* paired a piece on how wives could get their husbands more involved with the kids with a sidebar that listed five jobs mothers usually handle but fathers could do themselves. For instance: Pack the kid's lunch box occasionally, Pop.

Other list sidebars offer information related to the main article but not necessarily touched on in it. *Parents*, for example, listed the components of a good travel first aid kit in a sidebar to an article on traveling with young children.

THE NOT-ESPECIALLY-USEFUL (BUT-INTERESTING-NONETHELESS) LIST SIDEBAR

Not all lists are useful—some are merely fascinating. *Forbes* enhanced a report on the business of sports agents with a list of the world's forty highest paid athletes. The list may not have been especially useful to *Forbes'* audience of corporate executives, except perhaps in justifying their own salaries. But chances are they read it carefully. The highest paid athlete, you ask? Basketball player Michael Jordan, who was then earning an estimated $35.9 million.

THE QUIZ SIDEBAR

Sidebars that test a reader's knowledge have long been a magazine staple. The trick is to make them difficult enough to be challenging, but not so tough as to remind readers of a chemistry midterm.

Like list sidebars, quiz sidebars fall into two basic categories: the useful and the entertaining. There's no reason, of course, that a useful quiz can't be entertaining or that an entertaining quiz can't be useful. *Health* magazine, for example, ran a quiz on celebrities and their siblings with a more serious piece on the effect of birth order on personality. The quiz was entertaining, and it managed to illustrate some of the points of the larger article through well-known examples.

Then again, some entertaining quizzes are simply that. *Sky*, Delta Air Lines' in-flight magazine, celebrated the movie *Casablanca* with an article that included a sidebar for movie buffs. The title: "Here's Looking at You, Quiz."

THE "TERMS YOU NEED TO KNOW" SIDEBAR

Rather than clutter the main article with a lot of definitions, magazines will often pull out the key terms and define them in a separate glossary. *Better Homes and Gardens*, for example, ran a brief glossary on the different types of fats in food and in the human body as part of a health piece on low-fat dieting. *Martha Stewart Living* treated readers of its article on apple growing to an illustrated sidebar that identified thirty-seven different varieties of the fruit.

Writing a terms sidebar can be a challenge. The last thing you want to do is make a reader feel guilty or stupid for not already knowing what the terms mean. One magazine where I worked called glossary sidebars "refresher courses." That was our way of telling readers who once knew what a word meant but had since forgotten (and readers who never knew the term to begin with) that they had nothing to be ashamed of.

Runner's World took a similarly reader-friendly approach with a sidebar that accompanied an article on winter running apparel. The sidebar began: "We were confused about some of the technical terms used to describe the clothing we tested. And for good reason. Today's fabrics and fibers have become highly technical, and so have many of the terms used to name and de-

scribe them. So we waded through the mumbo jumbo and. . . ."
And so on, into the mumbo jumbo.

THE "YOU CAN DO IT, TOO" SIDEBAR

When a magazine article reports on people who are doing something interesting, a certain number of readers will decide they want to do that something, too. Hence, the "You Can Do It, Too" sidebar.

For example, *Worth* reported on shareholder activists who were challenging corporate boards of directors. A half-page sidebar offered, "A Primer for Activists." *Country Journal* reported on a successful food co-op in Vermont and, in a sidebar, told readers how they could start their own co-ops.

THE "WHERE TO GO FOR MORE INFORMATION" SIDEBAR

A close relative to the "You Can Do It, Too" sidebar, the "Where to Go" sidebar gives readers a list of resources to follow up on if they want to pursue a subject further.

New York Magazine, for example, ran a one-page sidebar on "Where to Turn for Help" with a report on child sexual abuse. The sidebar listed city and state agencies, treatment centers, self-help groups and useful books for both children and parents. *Mother Jones* offered a list of organizations for breast cancer patients alongside a writer's account of his mother's battle against the disease.

THE "QUESTIONS TO ASK" SIDEBAR

Another close relative of the "You Can Do It, Too" sidebar is the "Questions to Ask" sidebar. It doesn't tell readers where to go for more information, but what to say once they get there. The where-to-go stuff may be covered in the main article or in a separate sidebar.

Working Woman, for example, accompanied an article on "The Best Franchises for Women" with a list of questions to ask and documents to ask for before investing in a franchise. *Money* warned readers of the perils of dealing with a crooked or incompetent financial planner in its main article, then listed the "10 Questions You Should Ask on Your First Interview" in a sidebar.

79

THE "WHAT TO DO IF IT HAPPENS TO YOU" SIDEBAR

One way to give extra impact to a story is through a sidebar that tells readers that "it" could happen to them. The "it," of course, could be something cheery (like inheriting a '57 T-Bird) or something less so (like being attacked by rabid wolverines).

YM packaged a main article called "My Boyfriend Gave Me Herpes" ("He was older, handsome, sophisticated—and contagious") with a sidebar on how to tell if you have a sexually transmitted disease. *Essence* reported on stormy relations between black men and the police and included a sidebar, "If You Are a Victim of Police Brutality."

THE "IT HAPPENED TO ME" SIDEBAR

Magazines sometimes like to personalize their stories with a first-person account related to the main piece. If the writer originally became interested in the topic through a personal experience, that tale may make a good sidebar. Or, the writer may come across someone in the course of reporting the piece whose story is worth relating in an as-told-to format. Or, the magazine's editors may pair two different writers.

New Woman, for example, ran a feature on how the widely publicized Anita Hill hearings had reenergized the women's movement and added a sidebar on "The Day I Stood Up Against Harassment." The sidebar told the first-person story of a woman who, like Hill, said she had been sexually harassed.

THE "MEANWHILE, ELSEWHERE" SIDEBAR

Many times a magazine story will focus on what is only part of a larger trend. The magazine can give readers a sense of the big picture through sidebars.

For example, an article in *Popular Science* told readers about U.S. research into genetically engineered fruits and vegetables. A sidebar, meanwhile, looked at similar experiments in Mexico and Africa.

THE Q&A SIDEBAR

A question-and-answer sidebar allows a writer to explore in greater depth the thoughts of someone who figures in the main article or who isn't in the main article but has something noteworthy to say on the subject.

When *Rolling Stone* reported on the making of the movie *Malcolm X*, it interviewed actor Denzel Washington in an adjoining Q&A. By separating that material into a Q&A rather than trying to stuff it all into the main article, the magazine gave readers more insight into the actor's opinions.

THE RECIPE SIDEBAR

If you're profiling a celebrated chef or writing about a famous restaurant, a recipe might make a savory sidebar. *House & Garden* spiced its story about an island home off Puerto Rico with a page of local recipes.

THE "IT DIDN'T FIT IN THE MAIN ARTICLE" SIDEBAR

Many times a writer will come across material that doesn't fit the thesis of the main article but is just too interesting to leave out. Other times, editors will extract a chunk of an article that seems out of place and put it in a box under its own headline.

Some topics are so large or complex that the only proper way to come at them is from different angles, as if you'd been given a series of different assignments on the same broad topic. *Sunset* magazine, for example, offered a guided tour of the major airports of the Southwest and described how they were being redesigned for the future. Airport crime, an interesting but less-upbeat trend, was treated in a sidebar.

A sidebar can also present historical background without bogging readers down in material they may have read before. When *Woman's Day* profiled country singer Reba McEntire, for example, it managed to pack the previous eighteen years of her career into a one-column sidebar less than four inches long.

Finally, a side note on sidebars. The sidebar formats described here may be in vogue at the moment, but don't feel limited by them. A sidebar can take many forms. It might be a map, a graph, a poem, a song or something no writer before you has ever thought of.

In fact, you may find that editors allow you greater creative license with sidebars than they do with larger articles. So experiment, show off, enjoy yourself. And never fear that sidebars are less important to your editors or readers just because they aren't as verbose. The sidebar may be a small canvas, but it can also be a masterpiece.

14 SELLING YOUR VIEWS IN REVIEWS

If you were a reader of *Graham's Magazine* back in May 1842, you could have opened your latest issue to see what that brash young man Edgar Allen Poe thought of the new Nathaniel Hawthorne book, *Twice-Told Tales*. Poe and Hawthorne may no longer be with us, but reviewing remains a vital part of many magazines' editorial mix. Any number of magazines even have the word "review" in their names.

Today magazine writers review much more than books. Everything from *Snow White* to snow tires is fair game for evaluation in one publication or another.

So if you're the opinionated sort and would like to be paid for your opinions now and then, read on.

HOW TO BREAK IN

With most other kinds of magazine writing, the best way to approach an editor is with a specific idea for a piece. Even if he or she isn't interested in that idea, your query will show how well you understand that magazine's particular mission. With reviews, however, your best bet is often just to introduce yourself and to explain as persuasively as possible why you'd be a great choice as a reviewer. In the case of books, for example, many editors prefer to assign titles to reviewers rather than let reviewers suggest them, especially when they're working with someone they don't already know. You might want to review a book because the author is your best buddy—or your worst enemy.

To sell yourself as a reviewer, it's rarely enough to say you love books (or movies or whatever) and want to review them. You're better off selling yourself as an authority. So try to play up your expertise. If you're a science teacher, you could propose reviewing science books. If you're a salesperson, try books or audiotapes on selling. If you've had a fascination with monsters since childhood and have seen every Dracula movie ever made, ask to review a monster video. I once got an assignment to review a video on scouting by virtue of having been a Boy Scout (and not an especially good one) some twenty years earlier.

Clips of reviews you've published in other publications can help, too. Your writing style is especially important in reviewing. With other kinds of nonfiction, an editor might figure that even if your writing isn't up to par, he or she can at least take the information you provide and beat it into something publishable. With reviewing, though, you're selling a point of view and an ability to express it provocatively. Most editors would like to see some evidence of that before they take a chance on you as a reviewer.

What to do if you don't have any clips? Try to get some. Start with your local newspapers or other publications where the competition may be less keen. Try the trade journals in your field or the publications devoted to your hobbies. If you're a student, do reviews for the school paper or magazine. Almost anything is better than nothing.

Since it may be a while before an editor comes across an appropriate review project for you, it's smart to follow up every few months with a short note reminding him or her of your expertise and your interest in reviewing. That's also an opportunity to send along any new clips you've published in the meantime.

WHAT TO REVIEW
Among the many things magazines review today, you'll find:
- Books and books on tape
- Movies, both in theaters and on video
- Plays
- Music, both live performances and recordings
- Video games
- Restaurants
- Other products, from cosmetics to construction equipment

If you want to review any of the above for a particular magazine, first try to figure out whether it accepts freelance contributions in that category. For example, a magazine might have a regular movie reviewer but still be open to other writers for reviews of CDs or video games. In the case of products, you'll often find that magazines use staff writers as reviewers to avoid potential conflicts of interest. But if you're an avid nature photographer and would be the ideal person to review the latest lenses, there's no harm in proposing it.

THE REWARDS OF REVIEWING

Sad to say, but magazines frequently pay less for reviews than they do for other kinds of articles. For one thing, editors consider reviewing less work than conventional reporting: Sitting in a chair reading a murder mystery or in a movie theater watching a comedy somehow doesn't seem as arduous as poring through government records or chasing down real human beings to interview.

But if the money isn't all that spectacular, there are other perfectly good reasons for writing reviews. One is the opportunity to express your views in print. That's something you'll rarely get to do with other kinds of magazine articles, where you're expected to maintain at least the illusion of being an objective journalist no matter how strongly you may feel about a subject.

Some writers and writers' lives are also better suited to reviewing than to other kinds of magazine work. A writer who dreads calling strangers on the telephone to ask them questions may be much happier reading books and commenting on them. A part-time freelancer whose day job allows little time for reporting may enjoy watching and reviewing videos after work.

Perhaps the best reason of all, though, is that reviewing can be a lot of fun. If you love movies, books, videos or even construction equipment, reviewing allows you to get paid (albeit not grandly) for doing something you'd probably do anyway. If you review movies or theater, you'll usually get free tickets. If you review books or videos, you can often keep them when you're done. If you review construction equipment, though, I expect you'll have to give it back.

84

ONE SIMPLE SYSTEM

Because it's hard to make much of a living as a reviewer, most writers who do reviews learn to be fairly efficient about it. Here, for example, is the system I've used for years now in reviewing books.

1. Read with a sharp pencil (no. 2 or lighter) at the ready. When something strikes you as noteworthy, put a check mark in the margin. If you cringe at the idea of writing in books, or if you plan to recycle your review copies as birthday presents, keep your marks light, then go back later and erase them. No one will ever know.

2. When you finish the book, take out a sheet of lined paper and list all the page numbers where you made checks. Next to each page number, note what struck you as important. With all but the thickest books you should be able to confine your notes to a single page.

3. Now focus on your notes. Look for related ideas; something on page 238 may help explain a point on page 14. Look for contradictions. Make a rough outline for your review by assigning an order to the points you want to discuss.

4. As you write your review, try to work from your sheet of notes rather than from the book. Consult the book later to verify quotes or to check on other details.

Once you're done and your review is in the mail, file your notes along with your copy of the manuscript. If you need to refer to that book later for some future writing project, your notes will help you locate the relevant parts in a hurry—even if you erased all evidence of pencil marks.

When I've reviewed videos, I followed a similar system. I kept a clipboard in my lap for jotting down thoughts and noted in the margins about how many minutes into the video each part I wanted to comment on appeared. (If I'd been more obsessive about it, I could even have used the counter on the VCR to know exactly where those parts were.) When I later needed to go back to check on something, I could usually find it quickly. I never had to watch a video more than once, unless I enjoyed it so much that I wanted to.

SOME RULES FOR REVIEWERS

Fun though reviewing may be, it is also serious business. A favorable review can cause a magazine's readers to spend their time or money following your recommendation. An unfavorable one can do real harm to the people whose work you're passing judgment on.

Your best defense is to be fair. If you're reviewing a book, read it. Read the whole thing, even if you have formed an opinion by the time you reach page three. If you're reviewing a CD, listen to every track. If it's a video, keep that thumb off the fast-forward button. This may seem like obvious advice, but you'd be surprised how tempting it is, under certain circumstances, to skim or skip ahead. I speak as a man who once had to read and review an economics book while on his honeymoon.

Being fair doesn't necessarily mean being nice. If you think a book sucks, say so (though maybe not exactly in those terms). If a restaurant is good in some respects but weak in others, let your readers know. If a CD is a masterpiece in every possible respect, tell the world.

Whatever you do, try to be interesting. Only a small percentage of the readers of your review may see the movie, play the video game or whatever. But they did pay for the magazine your review appears in. So your piece has to provide information and entertainment in its own right. Make it a four-star winner.

15 REJECTION AND HOW TO DEAL WITH IT

Even though I've received my share of rejection slips in my years as a freelancer—and given other writers some of their share in my years as a magazine editor—I still don't find rejection easy to handle. It hurts, and I expect it always will.

I have, however, learned a few tricks to keep myself going, despite the occasional indignities of our otherwise happy trade. And unless you're some kind of armadillo-skinned writer who thrives on adversity, maybe they'll be of use to you, too.

REJECT REJECTION

First, it helps to remind yourself now and then that rejection isn't unique to the writing business. Ask any actor, any politician, anybody who sells anything for a living. Rejection is part of life. If you aren't rejected occasionally, you must be awfully good, or awfully lucky, or Warren Beatty. Or, more likely, you simply aren't trying hard enough.

Every writer I know, every writer I've ever read about, has had work rejected. James Thurber, to choose a writer almost at random, had twenty pieces rejected by *The New Yorker* before the magazine finally bought one. Once, when a piece didn't come back as quickly as usual, he went to the magazine's offices, hoping for good news. The piece, it turned out, had been temporarily buried on an editor's desk. The editor rejected that one in person. Somehow Thurber kept his sense of humor, a valuable trait not only for humorists but for writers of every stripe.

So what's the difference between the Thurbers of this world and writers that we've never heard of? For one thing, the Thurbers didn't give up. They kept writing, and they kept submitting. Who knows how many talented writers have quit just one story shy of acceptance.

That isn't to say you should lose sight of the odds against acceptance at certain publications. But never let those odds discourage you. A major magazine may receive two hundred queries or unsolicited manuscripts for every piece it publishes. Of the other 199, some undoubtedly come close to acceptance, whether their authors ever learn about it or not. So, if your piece is rejected, assume it just missed; that may not be true, but it will certainly do more for your morale than dwelling on the alternative. And if you have an idea you think is right for a certain publication, ignore the odds. Send it in. You have nothing to lose but some stamps.

One of the most prolific writers I've worked with told me that when he started out as a freelancer, he set a query quota for himself. Whatever else was going on in his life, he put five fresh queries into the mail each week. Not only did the sheer numbers of queries he sent out boost his odds of success, but having a quota to fill took some of the sting out of rejection. Even an unsuccessful query had done its bit in helping meet his weekly quota. Two suggestions if you want to try this technique yourself: (1) Don't send all those queries to the same editor or you'll wear out your welcome and the editor, and (2) Don't worry about how you'll handle the work if, through some quirk of fate, every single query results in an assignment. Nobody is that lucky.

Now and again, rejection can even be a positive experience. Really. You may learn something that will make your next piece better or easier to sell. Or you may simply learn that the editor you sent it to is a pig-headed Philistine you'll want to avoid in the future. When all else fails, consider the old saying, common among salespeople: "Every no brings you that much closer to a yes." So keep trying. Somewhere out there, a yes awaits you.

GET UNSTUCK

Forget everything you have ever heard or read about writer's block. There is no such thing as writer's block. Period. Well, maybe there is, but we're all better off if we pretend it doesn't exist. The freelancers I know simply don't have the luxury of waiting for their muse. They schedule the time to write a piece, then they sit down and write it, whether they're in the mood or not.

When writing doesn't come easily, the trick sometimes is simply to get started. You can always pitch those pages if they aren't up to your usual standards. And don't feel you have to begin at the beginning. Some writers like to start with the lead of their story and work down from there. But others simply start with whatever section comes most easily. They can always add the top of the piece later on. Do whatever works for you, and when that doesn't work, try something else. There are no rules, except the ones you make for yourself. You are your own boss.

Don't let the blank page or a ream of them overwhelm you. When I signed my first book contract, I gulped at the prospect of owing the publisher 50,000 words. Now, 50,000 words isn't exactly *Moby Dick*, but it was about 40,000 words longer than the longest piece I'd sold in my magazine career. The job seemed a lot more manageable after I'd done one very simple thing: I took ten manilla file folders and wrote a chapter title on each of them. When I finished, I still had those ten empty files to fill, but now I believed I could do it—one 5,000-word chapter at a time.

If you're ever hopelessly stuck, take a walk, make a cup of tea, play with the dog, call a friend. Or call a fellow writer for inspiration. I once asked my old friend Skip Cypert, the author of such motivational books as *Believe and Achieve* and *The Power of Self-Esteem*, how a motivational writer stays motivated.

"I have a system," he told me with a laugh. "First, sign the contract. Then, get the advance. Then, squander the advance. After that I know I have to write the book or they'll want their money back."

SAVOR YOUR SUCCESSES

You can't always control the way the world is going to treat you, but you can at least be gracious to yourself. Make time in your life to write. Create an environment that allows you to focus fully on your work. Look on the act of writing as its own reward, because sometimes it's the only reward we writers get.

The author and activist Saul Alinsky observed that little victories along the way will help keep groups of people working toward a major goal. So, however big your goals as a writer may be, make sure you have some small successes to celebrate in the meantime. If, for example, you aren't ready to sell to any of the big-league magazines—or if they don't have the good sense to recognize your readiness—offer to do a piece for your local weekly. Or write something gratis for your church newsletter. You'll have some fun, you'll sharpen your skills and you'll add another writing sample to your portfolio.

Before I sit down to write something new, I'll often reread one of my published pieces. It reminds me that whatever false starts and other difficulties lie ahead with the new piece, it too will probably see print one day.

If your own words don't inspire you, try a motivational book. Some classics are *The Power of Positive Thinking* by Norman Vincent Peale, *Think and Grow Rich* by Napoleon Hill, *How I Raised Myself From Failure to Success in Selling* by Frank Bettger and *The Autobiography of Benjamin Franklin* by you-know-who. To get the most out of these books and others of their kind, approach them like a Stephen King story—suspend all disbelief. Forgive their occasionally hokey tone. Ignore the fact that many of the people they hold out as shining examples are now seen as scoundrels. Just let the warm waves of inspiration wash over you. And then get back to work.

When you finish a manuscript and you're satisfied with it, buy yourself a candy bar. Pat yourself on the back. Go to the nearest mirror and admire your reflection. Ultimately, the piece may be accepted somewhere, or it may never be. But whatever its fate in the marketplace, if it's the best work you're capable of, you have every right to take pride in it.

Always remember: Unpublished pieces aren't failures. Unwritten pieces are.

16 FINDING TIME TO WRITE

What do magazine writers most like to gripe about? (Besides editors, I mean.) My guess would be not having enough time to write.

As a writer for some twenty years now, I may have tried every trick in the time-management book. I have set the alarm for 4 A.M. so I could write for an hour or two before getting showered and dressed for "work." I have stayed up way past my bedtime, burning the midnight cathode-ray tube. I have spent countless lunch hours with a sandwich in one hand and a pen in the other.

Most of what follows assumes that you'll be beginning your magazine-writing career as a part-timer. I'd recommend that course even if you have both the guts and the trust fund to go at it full time. Starting out part time is a good way to determine whether magazine writing is really for you, without cutting off all contact with the civilized world in the process. So here goes:

SEIZE THE DAY (OR AT LEAST A CHUNK OF IT)
If it's any consolation, all writers are really part-timers. Even those lucky enough to make a living with words still have to sleep, eat, get their teeth cleaned and fill out the occasional tax form.

Even if you have a full-time job, you probably have more hours at your disposal than you realize. Let's do the math. Say you work forty hours a week and spend another ten hours commuting. That's just fifty out of the 168 hours in any seven-day week. You've still got 118 hours to do with as you please. What's more, you can usually find fifteen minutes here, half an hour there within those fifty hours to write or at least to plan your next move.

That's not to say it's easy. For one thing, not all hours are created equal. If you're like most people, you probably think and write more clearly in the morning or afternoon than at the end of a long, tough workday. And if you have a family, there will be days when you want to go back to your manuscript and they want you to go to the mall. But with a little creativity and a lot of discipline you can make the time you do have really count for something.

Consider, for example, research. That's probably the biggest stumbling block for part-timers, particularly nonfiction writers. You may be happy to write from 10 P.M. to midnight, but chances are, the people you need to interview would rather talk to you between the hours of nine and five. If you can, try to schedule your interviews during whatever free time you can carve out during the day. For this chapter, I interviewed three writers at lunchtime and caught a fourth just after I got home from work. Because I live in the East and the fourth writer lives in the West, I was able to interview him at 7:30 my time, which was still just 4:30 his time. West Coast writers can take advantage of time-zone differences at the other end of the day, by making calls before work to people in the East. And they'll never know you're still in your pajamas.

Use spare vacation days. Jay Stuller, who works full time in Chevron Corporation's public affairs department and freelances for major magazines, tries to do most of his reporting by phone. But he saves some vacation time for stories that require out-of-town travel. An article on the Dallas-Ft. Worth Airport published in *Smithsonian Magazine*, for example, required five vacation days of reporting— and he never even got to leave the airport.

Learn the hours of your local public and university libraries. You can probably squeeze in some library time at lunch, after work or on weekends. In a pinch, librarians will sometimes look things up for you and answer your questions over the phone.

Build a decent reference collection at home. It doesn't have to be anything fancy. I still use a thirty-five-year-old set of Encyclopedia Britannicas. You can pick up a newer set (one that actually knows something about Watergate, Neil Armstrong and the Rolling Stones) for next to nothing at a used-book sale. Or, if you have a computer with a CD-ROM drive, you can get a nearly up-to-date encyclopedia on disk for about fifty dollars. For more about reference materials, see chapter twenty-one.

Hook up to the Internet. Access a ton of research material (newspapers, press releases, government data, you name it) twenty-four hours a day. You can also use it to connect with real people. That's useful when you need anecdotes for an article.

Interview by mail or E-mail. I've done that on rare occasions when I wasn't able to get to a subject by telephone. Some people will just ignore your correspondence or mean to answer you but never get around to it. Others will be so intrigued by your approach that they'll answer more thoughtfully than they would have on the phone. I've found this technique works pretty well with authors and others who are comfortable putting words on paper. It's also an option if you're shy by nature or easily tongue-tied.

GETTING DOWN TO BUSINESS

Once you've found some time to write, the next step is actually doing it. That, as we all know, can be the toughest job of all. There's something about having to concentrate on your writing that sets off every car alarm in a three-mile radius. The late Robert Benchley, whose skill as a humorist seems to have been matched only by his resourcefulness as a procrastinator, once offered this principle for getting things done: "Anyone can do any amount of work, provided it isn't the work he is supposed to be doing at that moment." So try to tune out the distractions and pretend that instead of writing, you really should be balancing your checkbook or waxing the car.

Hank Nuwer, a journalism teacher as well as a prolific magazine writer, told me his secret for juggling two full-time careers. "I set a pocket travel alarm to warn me when I need to make a phone call or must leave the office—say, to catch a plane," he said. "Once I set the alarm, I can concentrate fully on the work in front of me."

Business and management writer Peter Drucker recommends locking the door, disconnecting the phone and trying to work for a chunk of hours without interruption. Your goal, Drucker said, shouldn't be a first draft, but an even rougher "zero draft" that then be rewritten bit by bit in smaller blocks of time. Drucker offered this advice, incidentally, in a 1966 *Harper's Magazine* piece

93

called "How to Manage Your Time: Everybody's No. 1 Problem."
So the lack of time isn't exactly a new gripe.

Many writers find it helps to have a regular place to work. You don't necessarily need a corner office, or even an office, or for that matter even a corner. B.F. Skinner, the Harvard psychologist famed for "conditioning" rats to press levers and pigeons to play table tennis, conditioned himself to write for two hours every morning at a certain desk in his home. When he wanted to write a personal letter or pay bills, he did it in another part of the house.

Mystery writer Marissa Piesman trained herself to write on the subway, commuting to and from her job as an assistant state attorney general in New York City. "The subway is actually an easy place to concentrate," she told me. "It's so noisy that you don't get distracted by other people's conversations. And there's nothing much to see out the window." Writing in longhand on a steno pad, Piesman found that she could do four hundred words during her forty-five-minute morning commute—or a 2,000-word chapter every week. At the end of thirty-five weeks, she had a 35-chapter, 70,000-word book manuscript.

PICK YOUR TARGETS

One thing you learn quickly as a part-time writer is to choose your projects carefully. Don't, for example, propose an article in which you'd personally retrace the path of the Lewis and Clark expedition, unless your boss won't miss you for the next two years or so.

Rick Wolff, a full-time editor of business, sports and humor titles for Warner Books and frequent contributor to *Sports Illustrated*, offers some simple advice: "Try to pick subjects where you don't have to do much research because you already know the subject. Say you're an accountant whose hobby is gardening, and you're very proud of your pumpkins. It probably wouldn't make sense for you to try to write a novel about eighteenth-century Russia. But you could write about the best ways to grow pumpkins or how to keep racoons away from your crop." Wolff, a former minor league ballplayer, often writes about baseball.

If you aren't already an expert on, say, pumpkins or pinch hitting, that doesn't mean you can't write about them. Indeed, many free-lancers would argue that the joy of writing is in constantly learning new things. But it's also possible to waste months or even years researching some topic that no editor in the world will be interested in. A good middle ground, I've found, is to do enough research to write a persuasive query, then stop. If you get a go-ahead from an editor, you can invest more time. If you don't, chalk it up to your general education and move on to something else.

BEWARE THE BOSS

Being a part-time writer is a good way to get yourself in trouble with your full-time employer. As a general rule, try not to do anything that would give your employer the idea that your writing is more important to you than your full-time job (even if it is). For example, if you're writing a savage expose of your company or a comic novel whose most idiotic character bears a striking resemblance to your boss, it's probably not a good idea to do it on the office computer system or to leave the manuscript lying around your desk.

Jay Stuller, who has successfully juggled corporate work and part-time freelancing for twenty-two years, says, "I always do anything I'm supposed to do and then some." And he contends that his freelancing actually benefits his employer. "I learn a lot from the things I'm exposed to in doing outside projects," he says, "and I bring that back to the work I do here."

Your employer may have rules on part-time work, including writing. If you don't know, ask. And if you value your job, do your best to comply with them. To protect yourself, try to get any rules on outside writing *in* writing.

When all else fails, consider a pen name. That's the story behind Stanley Bing, a *Fortune* magazine columnist who also wrote for *Esquire* for more than a decade. Under his real name, Bing has a day job he characterizes as "a senior type for a vast multinational conglomerate." While Bing's secret identity isn't as secret as it once was, it does have its uses. "At the beginning it was a way of protecting me from my employers," he says. "Now it also serves to protect my employer." That is, the readers of Bing's column on office life or his book *Crazy Bosses* won't automatically assume he's writing about his particular vast multinational conglomerate.

Writing under a pen name does have a downside, of course. "You have to have a strong core ego," says Bing, "because you'll hear

95

people at the office praising something your alter ego just published, and you can't even tell them that was you."

SELLING YOURSELF

Selling is a tough job for any writer. And unfortunately, it doesn't get any easier when you're doing it part time. Not only do you have fewer hours to research new markets and polish your queries, but the mere fact that you're a part-timer will sometimes be held against you. One magazine editor I know told me that she won't assign anything to part-time freelancers, simply because she can't count on them to be available at a moment's notice to answer questions or do more work on a manuscript.

So what's a part-timer to do? Some editors may disagree with me, but I don't think it's necessary to advertise your part-time status. Don't lie about it if you're asked, of course, but unless your full-time job is relevant to the story you're pitching, there's no compelling reason to bring it up. Many editors don't care whether you're full time or part time—as long as you can deliver on time.

Stanley Bing says it's particularly important for part-timers to cultivate relationships with editors. "Get to know as many editors as you possibly can," he says. "Develop long-term relationships with them. That way you're not always pitching ideas to editors who don't know you. And never say no, no matter how busy you are."

One of the best part-time gigs I've had in nearly two decades of freelancing was a series of author interviews I did for seven years for a slick quarterly magazine published by a big accounting firm. The interviewing was fun, the editing was top-notch and the money wasn't bad either. Most important, I could schedule the interviews (and the weekends for transcribing the tapes and writing them up) well in advance, to avoid any conflicts with my full-time work.

Bing has another bit of shrewd advice for part-timers: "Charge enough to make it worth the invasion of your life space," he says. "Don't work for cheap."

To which I'd only add: unless you really want to. Because when you're a part-time writer, you're your own boss. More so, in fact, than all but the richest of full-time writers. So whether it's fortune, fame or simply the pleasure of a well-crafted page that motivates you, go for it. As for me, I've got to get ready for, ahem, "work."

96

17 MONEY MATTERS FOR WRITERS

The poet and occasional magazine writer Robert Frost once observed that poets sometimes had to be even more businesslike than businessmen because "their wares are so much harder to get rid of."

Magazine writers—at least those of the prose nonfiction variety—probably don't face as much sales resistance as the average poet. But being businesslike never hurts. In this chapter, we'll look at some of the business basics no writer can afford to ignore.

GETTING PAID

If you're lucky, most of the magazines you write for will pay you promptly, if not always as generously as you might wish. Magazines do, however, have varying arrangements for paying writers, a detail that should be spelled out in your contract. The two arrangements you'll most likely encounter are:

Payment on acceptance. This means when the magazine receives a manuscript from you that the editor deems acceptable, you will be paid. Don't expect a check by return mail, however. A magazine's accounting department will usually take at least a week to send you one. Delays of thirty days are all too common, and some magazines will stall you for ninety days or more.

If you aren't paid within a reasonable time after acceptance— and you'll begin to get a feel for what's reasonable after you've worked with a given magazine for a while—a gentle reminder to your editor, by phone or letter, isn't out of line. Some battle-hardened freelancers I know skip the editor reminder and call the magazine's accounting department directly. If they're going to get into a screaming match with someone, they figure, better the accountant than their editor.

Payment on publication. This is a far worse arrangement for the writer. If the magazine holds your piece for a year before running it, you'll wait a year for your money, plus perhaps another ninety days while the accounting department dillydallies in writing the check. If the magazine never publishes your piece, you may never be paid. In short, avoid magazines that pay on publication if at all possible.

Contracts are full of other provisions too, of course. We'll look at more of them in chapter eighteen.

GETTING PAID . . . MORE

In the beginning, you may be grateful to be paid anything at all for your work. I can remember getting checks for fifteen dollars and twenty-five dollars and not believing my good fortune. But after you've been at it for a while, you may rightly wonder why you aren't being paid more.

One way to make that happen is simply to ask for more. Editors usually have some leeway in their budgets, though often less than writers suspect. An editor who offers you, say, fifty cents a word for a piece may be able to bump that up to seventy-five cents, but it's unlikely he or she could go to two dollars. Unless you're already an established writer with lots of work coming your way, you may not want to ask for more money the first time you work with an editor. But once you've built a relationship, there's no harm in it. Probably the worst thing that can happen is the editor will say no.

Whether or not you've worked for a magazine before, it's reasonable to ask for more money if the editor decides to expand the scope of the project after you agreed to it. For example, if you've delivered a finished piece and the magazine now wants a new five hundred-word sidebar, most editors will understand if you ask for an additional fee.

It's rarely a good idea, however, to try to renegotiate your fee on a piece that's basically what the editor assigned, even if it ended up requiring more work than you anticipated. That's a risk freelancers are expected to take. As you gain experience, you'll develop a sixth sense about which projects are readily doable and which are doomed to be black holes of effort and energy. Until then, best of luck. And if it's any consolation, some projects will turn out to be even easier than you anticipated.

TAXES

When you start a business of your own—whether you're a writer, plumber or palm reader—you enter a new world of tax considerations. Since tax laws are always changing, this section will only hit the high points. For more current and specific advice, grab one of the popular annual tax references, such as *The Ernst & Young Tax Guide*, or check with an accountant.

Deductions. If you're a professional writer, even a part-time one, the tools of your trade are deductible against your income on a tax form you'll soon get to know well. It's called Schedule C—Profit or Loss From Business. So, for example, if you earn one thousand dollars from your magazine articles and spend two hundred dollars on writing supplies, you'll owe taxes only on your net income of eight hundred dollars. It's even possible to claim a loss some years if you spend more than you take in.

What's deductible? Here are some examples:

- Batteries for your pencil sharpener, tape recorder or laptop computer
- Books and magazines needed for your work
- Computers and computer software (if you use them for writing as opposed to storing casserole recipes or playing Donkey Kong)
- Dues for writers groups you belong to
- Paper, envelopes, notepads and notebooks
- Pencils, pens, erasers, etc.
- Photocopying
- Postage and other shipping costs
- Tapes for recording interviews
- Telephone calls
- Transportation to interviews with subjects or meetings with editors. If you use you car rather than public transportation, you can deduct the expense on a per-mile rate or according to a more complicated formula involving the actual cost of owning and maintaining your car. The per-mile rate at this writing

is 32.5 cents, but it changes every couple of years, so be sure to look it up again when the time comes.

- And just about everything else you buy to do your work as a writer—every paper clip, staple, rubber band and all the rest. Some of these items may seem insignificant, but believe me, they add up.

Saving for retirement. One of the great things about freelance writing is you can continue to work well into your retirement years if you feel like it. Another of those great things is that having your own business makes it easier to save for retirement while you're still working.

For example, you may be able to contribute a portion of your freelance income to a retirement vehicle such as a SEP-IRA (SEP stands for Simplified Employee Pension) or a Keogh Plan. The maximum amounts you can kick in vary from plan to plan, as do other assorted rules. But they all allow you to defer paying taxes on the money you contribute and on your account's investment earnings. The government gets its cut when you eventually withdraw your money.

As with taxes, this is an area that changes frequently, so be sure to check on the latest rules before you make any moves. The IRS offers free publications that aren't much on looks but do explain things pretty clearly. Call 800-TAX-FORM or visit the IRS Web site at www.irs.ustreas.gov.

Recordkeeping. When the time rolls around to prepare your income tax return for the year, you'll be glad if you kept a good record of your freelance expenses. You'll be doubly glad if the IRS ever calls you in for an audit.

Your recordkeeping system can be as elaborate as you'd like, but you'll save time if you keep it relatively simple. I use a stenographer-size notebook to record all my freelance expenses, as well as the occasional check. I stuff my receipts in a 9″ × 12″ envelope.

How long do you need to keep receipts? The conventional wisdom is at least three years. That's the length of time the IRS normally has in which to audit you; if the IRS suspects that you've seriously underreported your income, however, the limit expands to six years. In the case of tax fraud, there's no limit at all. My advice:

MONEY MATTERS FOR WRITERS

Save your records forever. The IRS may never show any interest in them, but they could be a lot of fun for you to sit down with ten or twenty years from now, as you relive your early freelance adventures. And who knows: If you really hit it big, private collectors and university libraries may one day be bidding for them.

INSURANCE
Your insurance needs as a magazine writer are less complicated than if you were, say, a professional bungee jumper. But it's worth a quick call to the agent who handles your homeowner's or renter's policy to make sure you're adequately covered. In particular, ask about:

Property coverage for your computer or other gear. Your homeowner's policy may already cover you for a certain amount, such as $2,500. But if your equipment would cost more than that to replace, you may want to buy additional coverage.

Liability. If a customer or supplier is injured at your home, you could be held financially responsible. Most writers I know don't have a lot of visitors during the day—if they did, they'd never get any work done. But if, for example, you also write press releases for local businesses and often see clients in your home, check your liability coverage. You may be able to increase the liability limits on your current plan by purchasing what's called an umbrella policy. Or you may need separate business liability coverage.

SAVING MONEY ON SUPPLIES
You don't need a lot of equipment to go into business as a writer. In fact, before the advent of typewriters and then computers, about all a writer required was a sharp pencil. These days you'll need a few more things, but you don't have to spend a lot of money on them if you know where to shop. Here are three money-saving tips:

1. Buy used. There's a huge market out there of used desks, filing cabinets and other office stuff. Used gear may cost a fraction of what you'd pay for the same items new. And sometimes it's sturdier, too. Watch your local want ads or check the yellow pages.

2. Find the nearest discount office-supply store. Chains like Office Depot and Staples often have great deals on paper, envelopes and other essentials. Warehouse stores like Sam's Club and PriceCostco are another option, though their selection isn't as wide.

3. Borrow if you can. Your public library probably has a lot of the books, magazines and other reference materials you need. And its prices are hard to beat.

Finally, remember the words of the immortal magazine publisher Ben Franklin: Time is money[1]. As long as you can afford it without denying your family the basic necessities, don't skimp on gear that will give you more time to write or that will make the writing time you already have more productive. Having your own photocopier or fax machine, for example, will allow you to focus on your writing when you might otherwise be watching the clock worrying about what time the copy or fax shop closes.

---

[1] Historical footnote: Franklin conceived the first magazine in the colonies, in 1740, though a rival publisher managed to get his own first issue out a few days ahead of Franklin's. *The General Magazine*, as Franklin called his periodical, published six issues and went out of business in 1741. Franklin's rival lasted for three issues.

18 KNOW YOUR RIGHTS

Once upon a time, a deal between a magazine editor and a writer might have gone something like this:

> Editor: "We'll pay one hundred dollars to use your article."
> Writer: "Uh, OK."

Today, whatever the editor and writer say to each other is likely to be followed up by a multipage contract full of clauses and subclauses and lots of words like "whereas" and "wherefore." When I recently looked back through a book on freelance writing I read twenty years ago, I noticed that it didn't even mention magazine contracts. Times have changed and, in this case, not necessarily for the better.

You don't have to go to law school to be a writer today, although it probably wouldn't hurt. You do, however, need to learn a few more things about contracts than you might have had to a generation ago.

As you read this chapter, bear in mind that magazine contracts, like other contracts, are often negotiable. In fact, it's a badly kept secret in the magazine business that some publishers even keep several contracts on hand—one for eager novices who would sign just about anything to sell a story and a fairer version for experienced writers who know what they're doing. So if a magazine offers you a contract that you consider unreasonable, there's no harm in trying to negotiate better terms. And if the magazine refuses to budge, you may want to take your talents elsewhere.

RIGHTS AND THE WRITER

As a magazine writer, you're likely to encounter all sorts of different rights arrangements. But the two most basic variations are one-time rights and all rights.

One-time rights. When you sell a magazine piece, the editor may ask for first North American serial rights. This simply means that you're selling the magazine the right to publish your article for the first time in North America. Serial, incidentally, is just a fancy name for magazine.

Once your article has been published, you may be able to sell it elsewhere. The next magazine's contract may call for second-serial or one-time rights. Again, you'll simply be selling the magazine the right to publish your piece once, and you'll be able to sell it again if you wish.

All rights. Some magazines, though, are not satisfied with the right to run your article once. They want to be able to use it in another magazine, a book, an audiotape or videotape or, as the lawyers like to put it, "any medium now known or hereafter developed." Such magazines may tell you that they are buying all rights or else use the terms "work for hire" or "work made for hire." By whatever name, the bottom line is the same: Once the magazine has paid for your article, it belongs to the magazine, not to you.

Obviously, first North American serial rights or some other one-time rights deal is the best arrangement for you as a writer. There will come times, however, when you'll be faced with an all-rights contract that a magazine refuses to change. Should you take it or leave it? That depends, I think, on the article. If it is aimed at a narrow audience (and therefore unlikely to sell to another magazine) or if it's newsy (and therefore likely to go stale before you could possibly resell it), you may want to grit your teeth and sign, assuming the pay and other terms are fair. However, if you believe you could resell the article or, for example, include it in a book you've got in mind, you may want to say no thanks. Remember, though, that even if you sell all rights to a piece, there is nothing to stop you from writing another piece on the same topic.

Those are the two rights arrangements you're most likely to encounter these days. Here are some further complications:

Electronic rights. Many magazines now have electronic versions of themselves on the World Wide Web and commercial on-line services. If you sign an all-rights contract, a magazine can post your article on-line at will. Otherwise, the magazine will probably make some provision for buying electronic rights from you. Some magazines expect you to turn over electronic rights for free, arguing that a Web site is just an extension of the magazine or that they don't make any money at it anyway. Other magazines will offer you a small fee if your article is used on-line.

Some writers, sensing that electronic publishing may one day be far more profitable, balk at giving away electronic rights or selling them cheaply. A shrewd compromise a number of writers are now striking is to sell their electronic rights for a modest fee (say, fifty dollars) but only for a limited period of time (say, one year). That way, if the electronic publishing business should suddenly turn wildly profitable, the writer can renegotiate a higher fee.

Reprint rights. If a newspaper, for instance, wants to reprint a piece of yours, the magazine's contract may cut the magazine in for a chunk of the reprint fee. A 50/50 split between writer and magazine is fairly common, but you may be able to ask for more or even cut the magazine out of reselling your piece entirely. If you sold all rights, of course, the split is more likely to be 0/100, with guess who getting the 100.

Indemnification clauses. In recent years, some magazines have added clauses to their contracts that hold the writer financially responsible for any legal actions that result from an article's publication. Since magazine companies tend to be richer than most writers, you may wonder why a magazine would expect you to pay its legal bills. Good question. Some magazines will tell you that such clauses are simply meant to scare the writer into being extra careful. And scare, they do: Quite a few writers refuse to sign contracts with indemnification clauses. If you can't get a magazine to strike its indemnification clause, and you see any possibility of legal trouble down the road, you may not want to sign that contract.

One final hint: Even if you have written for a particular magazine before, be sure to read each new contract it sends you. Magazines revise their contracts periodically and rarely for the benefit of their writers.

19 WHAT TO DO AFTER YOUR ARTICLE IS PUBLISHED

Once the magazine with your article has hit the newsstands, your job may be over in the strictest sense. But your opportunities aren't. In this chapter we'll look at a few ways you can use your published pieces to make yourself better known, better off and maybe even a better magazine writer.

WELCOME TO THE PR MACHINE

Large magazines often have full-time public relations people whose job is to put the magazine on a pedestal and keep it there. These days that usually means getting the magazine's editors and writers on television and radio to promote the latest issue. So if you write a piece for a major magazine, you may soon find yourself as interviewee rather than interviewer. Unless you're an exhibitionist by nature, that may seem a little scary, at least at the beginning.

The first time I was going to be on the radio, I spent an entire Sunday asking myself questions and then answering them into a tape recorder. I was nervous right up until I went on the air, but once the interview started, I was just fine. I found I actually enjoyed it, and when the interviewer said it was time to go, I wanted to stay on and keep babbling. Chances are, you'll do at least as well as I did, as long as you know your subject.

To refresh my memory of a piece I may have written months earlier, I try to reread the article an hour or two before the interview and use a yellow highlighting pen to mark the most important points I may be asked about.

Even more useful, I've found, is making a list of the three or four most important points I want to get across, whether the interviewer asks me about them or not. People who are interviewed a lot use a technique that's sometimes called "bridging" to give the answer they want to give regardless of what the question was.

Suppose, for example, that you have written an article about remarkable new advances in fire-fighting technology, and for some reason the show's host wants to talk about the Great Chicago Fire of 1871. Here's how the conversation might go if you didn't know how to twist it around to the subject of your article:

> Host: "Mrs. O'Leary's cow—guilty or not guilty?"
> You: "Um. . . ."
> Here, instead, is how you might bridge back to your article:
> Host: "Mrs. O'Leary's cow—guilty or not guilty?"
> You: "I suppose historians will be debating that one for a long time, Chuck. But there's no debate that today's new firetrucks can handle blazes that would have been impossible to stop just a few years ago. For example. . . ."

The amazing thing, you'll find, is that Chuck probably doesn't care at all about whether you answered his question. His main interest is in keeping the show moving. Most radio interviewers are perfectly happy for you to take the conversation and run with it. For more (and better) examples of controlling an interview, catch any presidential press conference.

One of the nicest things about radio interviews is that they're usually done over the telephone rather than in a studio. Try to think of it as a phone conversation between you and the interviewer, and forget that a few thousand other people may be listening. And since the audience can't see you, you can be in your pajamas or your jockey shorts if you see fit, even if you're expounding on the latest in elegant evening wear.

Television is a little trickier, although most of the rules for radio still apply. If a magazine wants you to appear on TV and you've never done it before, ask if you could have some coaching before you go on. Magazines often use freelance TV coaches, typically someone with years of experience in the industry, to help writers come across more effectively on camera. If you can't get any help, just try to be yourself. Make a list of the two or three points you most want to cover and review it before you go on. Try to be upbeat, and keep your fingers out of your nose. Odds are, you'll do great, and in any case, it will be over in a few minutes.

PUBLICIZING YOURSELF

Smaller magazines may have little or no publicity machinery, so if you want to get some attention for your article (or for yourself), you're on your own. Here are some of the things you can try.

First, keep a list of people who have interviewed you in the past. In the case of radio or television, jot down the names of the producers as well as the on-air folks. When you have another article out that may be appropriate, send it to them, along with an offer to come back on the show. A follow-up phone call in a few days can help too.

Send a copy to your local newspaper. If it's local enough (and not *The New York Times*, say) it may be interested in the fact that a local resident has published something in a national magazine. Don't forget weeklies and free newspapers.

Send a copy to other publications that may be interested in your accomplishments, such as alumni magazines and the journals of any professional organizations you belong to.

What is the point of publicity? Good question. The bulk of any interviews you do on some magazine's behalf may sell a few more copies (and impress your loved ones), but they're unlikely to make you rich or famous. It's also rare for a magazine (or a radio or TV station) to pay you for your efforts. Indeed, the time you spend on publicity is time you won't be able to devote to your writing. That said, I think it's almost always worth it. For one thing, becoming comfortable on radio and television is a skill that may benefit you later in your writing career, especially if you write a book. For another, helping the magazines you write for get some attention will make you a more marketable commodity and possibly lead to further assignments down the line. And finally, it's enlightening to experience an interview from the other side of the microphone or notepad. Seeing your name misspelled on a television screen or your quotes mangled in print will give you a new appreciation of how nonjournalists sometimes view us.

MAKE SURE THE PEOPLE WHO HELPED YOU GET A COPY

Many magazines routinely send complimentary copies to the people featured in their pages. Others are too busy, too lazy or just too cheap.

I have often bought copies of magazines with my stories in them and sent them at my own expense to people I've quoted. For one thing, it's just courteous. Unless your interviewees subscribe to the magazine, they may never see the article. For another thing, you may want to interview those people again someday.

Sending a copy to each of your sources also allows you to correct any errors that the magazine, not you, was responsible for: "P.S.— My apologies for the unfortunate reference to you on page 48. I had written *distinguished philanthropist*, which the editors seem to have changed to *disgusting philanderer*. Sorry."

One exception: If you do refer to people as disgusting philanderers and the like, you may want to skip sending them copies. They'll hear soon enough, and there's no sense giving them your home address.

RESELLING YOUR WORK

If you own the rights to your published article, you may want to try selling it to another magazine or newspaper. Some writers earn a good share of their income this way.

But don't get your hopes too high. More and more magazines now insist on all rights or similarly restrictive contracts, leaving writers with nothing much to resell. Magazines are also becoming increasingly specialized in what they cover, making it less likely that any given article will fit another magazine's needs.

You may find, however, that you can dip back into your interview notes and other research and create an essentially new article for a different magazine. For example, an interview with a prominent fish expert could lead to a piece for a tropical fish magazine on how he displays his finned friends and one for a scuba diving magazine on how he collects them.

BUILDING A KILLER CLIP FILE

A "clip" is magazine jargon for a published article. So when editors ask to see your clips, they don't mean the little metal objects you use to keep papers together.

Every article you publish enlarges your clip file, allowing you a greater selection of things to show off your talents to prospective editors. A few clips from prestigious magazines can open more doors than a hotel doorman.

In other words, don't just file your article away and forget it. Consider it a resource that can help you win future assignments.

As you complete more and more of those assignments, your clips may become a little harder to keep track of. You'll probably remember for life the first few pieces you publish. After you've done a couple dozen, you'll find they begin to fade. I once worked with a prolific magazine and newspaper columnist who swore he couldn't remember what he wrote last week, let alone a few years ago. And he was otherwise as sharp as they come.

So at some point you'll probably need a system for filing your published pieces away for easy retrieval. One solution is to file by article type. For example, put personality profiles in one folder, travel pieces in another, book reviews in yet another and so on. Or photocopy your clips and stick them in three-ring binders, each devoted to a different type of article. So when you're pitching a travel piece, for example, you'll be able to quickly pull out a few relevant samples, photocopy them and attach them to your query.

Some writers you encounter will have more elaborate filing systems, practically to the point of inventing their own personal Dewey decimal systems. My advice is: Do whatever it takes to keep your clips handy, but don't go nuts. Your job as a writer isn't to catalog your past glories. Your job is to write lots of great new stuff. And if you do it well enough, future generations of librarians and archivists will be more than happy to get it properly organized.

One last tip: If you write for newspapers or for magazines with really crummy paper, make a few photocopies before your article gets too old. Even tucked away in a dark filing cabinet, some clips turn yellow and fade, making them much harder to copy later on.

BUT BEFORE YOU FILE YOUR ARTICLE AWAY . . .

Read it. Even if the magazine sent you prepublication galleys to show how your piece was edited, you may find that other changes were introduced before the piece finally went to press. Reading your article in print has countless benefits. For one thing, you may catch errors that were no fault of yours. In that case, a polite letter to your editor isn't out of line. A responsible magazine (and, yes, there still are some) will run a correction in a later issue if the mistake is serious enough.

More often, though, you'll learn something useful about the editing process at that magazine. Some of the changes the editors made to your article may seem dumb to you, and you may be right. Editors aren't infallible, and some are downright dangerous. If a magazine has truly butchered your work, you probably don't want to write for it again, at least until it gets a new cast of editors.

But you may also see changes that you have to admit, all ego aside, represent improvements to your original. Did an editor find a way to tighten your lead paragraph to get the reader into the story more quickly? Was a long, boring quote paraphrased into something better? Was some dense, hard-to-follow paragraph untangled and simplified? By seeing how an editor sharpened your prose, you're in a better position to do it yourself next time around.

Falling somewhere between butchery and beautiful cosmetic surgery will be editorial changes that may merely baffle you. Some of these will be nothing more than your editor's personal whims. The famed editor and writer H.L. Mencken, for example, was said to have inserted whole phrases of German into the pieces he edited, much to the consternation of writers who didn't know a word of the language. But other changes will represent the particular tone and voice that the magazine is striving for. Pick up on those clues, and you'll be on your way to becoming a valued and regular contributor. "Read the magazine" is time-honored advice for writers who want to sell to a particular market. "Read your piece in the magazine" may be better advice yet.

20 THE WRITER'S REFERENCE SHELF

Most writers I know love to be surrounded by books—shelves and shelves of them if at all possible. Books are useful for reference or inspiration, handsome as wall decor and pretty effective as sound-proofing against that jerk next door with the loud stereo.

The books you really need to do your work as a writer, though, could fit on a pretty short shelf. Here are seven of them.

SEVEN BOOKS EVERY WRITER NEEDS

Dictionary. Even in this age of computer word processing programs with spell checkers, a dictionary can be handy to have around. Sure, a spell checker can save you the indignity of misspelling the word *gourmand*. But a dictionary can tell you that the word you really want is *gourmet*. Any decent dictionary will do. One you see around many magazine offices is *Merriam-Webster's Collegiate Dictionary*.

Thesaurus. No offense, Peter Mark Roget, but I think a thesaurus often does more harm than good. If your brain is in decent working order, all the words you need should be in there already. A thesaurus may provide you with fancier synonyms, but most of the time the word you think of first will be simplest and best for the job.

A thesaurus can, however, be useful if you can't come up with that simple word you're groping for. (And don't worry, it happens to all of us.) It can also be helpful if you're writing a title for your story and want to play around with a lot of different words that would get your point across. The thesaurus I've found most useful is *Webster's New World Thesaurus*, edited by Charlton Laird (Macmillan).

Style book. When magazine editors refer to style, they don't mean dressing like the Duchess of Windsor or dancing like Fred Astaire. They mean the way the magazine handles matters like capitalization, italics, abbreviations and so forth. For example, one magazine may refer to St. Louis, Missouri; another to St. Louis, Mo.; and a third simply to St. Louis, figuring everybody knows what state St. Louis is in.

Large publications often have their own style books for the use of their writers and editors, and some even publish them for all the world to see. *The New York Times* and *U.S. News & World Report*, for example, have both published style books.

Smaller publications may use one of the more common style books, such as *The Associated Press Stylebook and Libel Manual*, *The Chicago Manual of Style*, or *Words Into Type*. They may also have a sheet of two of rules that supplement—or even contradict—the style book's guidelines. Often these rules amount to little more than a particular editor's whims or idiosyncrasies. I once worked at a magazine where the editor forbade the use of the word "rip-off"; the next magazine I worked for didn't hesitate to use it, even on the cover. Neither was right or wrong; it was simply a matter of style.

So do you need a shelf of style books for each of the magazines you want to write for? Thankfully, no. While it would be helpful to editors (and demonstrate what a conscientious person you are) if you try to follow their magazines' style, you can learn a lot simply by scanning a copy of the magazine for instances similar to the one you are facing. For example, if you're listing four things in a sentence, does the magazine handle it this way:

". . . red, orange, yellow, and green . . ."

or this way:

". . . red, orange, yellow and green . . ."

113

That final comma in the series (or the lack of it) is one of the things magazines will do differently. And you'll save some copyeditor the trouble of putting a comma in (or taking one out) if you do whatever the magazine normally does. Beyond that, though, it's really the copyeditor's job to make sure such nuances are tended to.

If you have room on your shelf and in your budget for a style book, buy *The Associated Press Stylebook and Libel Manual*. It's one that many magazines and newspapers follow, and it also has a lot of worthy advice on writing clearly and staying out of trouble.

Books of quotations. Like a thesaurus, a quotation book can be hazardous to your writing. Once you've read what Charles Dickens, for example, had to say on your subject, you may be tempted to:

a. Quote him for your lead, or

b. Give up writing, since Dickens seems to have said everything worth saying 130 years ago.

Either would be a mistake.

The problem with books like *Bartlett's Familiar Quotations* is that much of what they contain is just that—familiar. Many readers will have read those quotes before, and most editors will have used more pencil lead than they care to think about scratching them out.

How many times have you as a reader encountered some tired line attributed to Ben Franklin, Dorothy Parker or Yogi Berra? If you've seen a quotation a dozen times, your editor has probably seen it five dozen times. And neither of you should have to see it again.

So if you're to avoid familiar quotations, what's the point of owning a quotation book? A couple of reasons, I think. For one thing, you can sometimes find inspiration in what other writers have said on your subject, and a quotation book is a convenient gathering place for such lofty thoughts. You may also find people you interview quoting some famous utterance, and a quotation book will help you determine if they got it right.

Yet another reason is that you may find a still-unfamiliar quotation that you can use or a familiar one that you can put a fresh spin on or use to introduce new information. For example, I violated my own rule and quoted Ben Franklin in chapter seventeen of this book. But I did it for a reason, namely to sneak in the fact that among

Franklin's many other achievements, he founded one of the earliest magazines in America.

Encyclopedia. An encyclopedia is a great time-saver when you need to check on a date in history, confirm the spelling of some dead king's name or remind yourself which planet is closest to our sun (it's Mercury, my old Britannica informs me). Unless you're writing about history, though, encyclopedias are less useful for other kinds of magazine article research. Magazines want timely information, and much of what you'll find in an encyclopedia is already out of date. So there's no substitute for getting on the phone and calling the best authorities you can find on your subject.

You may already have an encyclopedia around the house that will serve your purposes. If not, you can often pick up an old set at a used-book sale for twenty-five dollars or less. Encyclopedias on CD-ROM run about fifty dollars. A handy one-volume book is *The Concise Columbia Encyclopedia*, which lists for about twenty dollars in paperback.

Almanac. A reasonably current almanac is a good, cheap (about ten dollars) adjunct to an encyclopedia. Though almanacs and encyclopedias cover much of the same ground, an almanac is likely to be stronger on government statistics, as well as on trivia like entertainers' birthdays that encyclopedias tend to ignore.

Atlas. Encyclopedias often have maps that will show you the ancient boundaries of the Ottoman Empire or remind you where the U.S.S.R. used to be. But if you're writing about the United States, there's no substitute for a good road atlas. An atlas will tell you, for example, how far Cincinnati is from Portland, Oregon (2,347 miles). You can also use it to check the names of towns far too small to merit mention in the encyclopedia. A good road atlas usually costs fifteen dollars or less; you can sometimes find last year's model on sale for just a few bucks.

21 HOW TO SPEAK "MAGAZINE"

Like any other trade, magazines have their own jargon. Some of the words that writers and editors toss around come from old printing processes, some from Latin and some from who-knows-where. This list, though far from complete, can help you speak magazine like a native. And if some editor orders you to "kill that widow," you won't end up doing anything you'd regret.

Add. More material added to an article.

Advertorial. An advertiser-sponsored section in a magazine that may at first glance look like legitimate editorial material.

Art. Artwork or photography that illustrates a magazine piece.

Back of book (sometimes abbreviated as BOB). The rear of the magazine, often the home of its less popular departments.

Bank. A supply of finished articles the magazine can draw on in putting together issues. Most magazines never establish a very large backlog of material, both because articles are perishable and because editors are often scrambling to fill the issue at hand.

Bleed. A photo or other type of art that goes all the way to the edge of the page.

Book. In editor jargon, magazines are often referred to as "books"—as in "back of book" and "front of book."

Bullet. A typographical device often used to begin each item in a list. A typical bullet looks like this: •.

Byline. Your name on a story, preferably spelled right.

Church and state. The editorial and advertising departments, respectively, of a magazine. Note that editorial is the holy one.

Clips. Copies of previously published pieces. An editor may invite you to "send me some clips" in order to see the kinds of things you've written in the past. Clips can be actual clippings or photocopies of them. Hint: the less unwieldy, the better. Clips copied onto normal 8½″ × 11″ paper are ideal.

Closing. The last stage of putting a magazine together before it goes to press, often characterized by long hours and much complaining.

Comp list. A list of people who get a magazine for free ("comp" is short for "complimentary"). An editor who puts your name on the comp list is one who wants to keep doing business with you.

Consumer magazine. One people read for personal, rather than work, reasons.

Contributing editor. Usually a writer, rather than an editor, who contributes regularly to that publication but is not a member of its full-time staff. The title of contributing editor is largely honorary and seldom involves any money beyond what the freelancer gets paid for actually writing. But it looks good on a resume and hey, in this business you take your honors where you can get them.

Correspondent. Often a freelancer who covers a certain geographical or subject area. See also *Stringer*.

Cutline. A photo caption. Photos and other illustrations were once referred to as "cuts," though that term has pretty much faded into magazine memory.

Deadline. The due date for a magazine article. The word comes from a line drawn once around military prisons beyond which wandering prisoners would be shot. Though you're unlikely to be shot for missing a deadline, your reputation with that magazine may be. As one of my journalism professors once scrawled on the chalkboard, "Deadlines are sacred."

Deck. The large type, usually below a headline, that helps readers understand what the story is going to be about. Editors tend to write these themselves, though you may occasionally be asked to take a whack at it.

Department. An ongoing, usually short, section of a magazine.

Feature. A magazine article.

Filler. Short material used to fill a column of type when an article comes up short.

117

Flack. A not-very-nice term for a public relations person.

Folio. The line of type on a magazine page that gives the page number, the name of the magazine and the date of the issue.

Four color. Magazine pages that are printed in what we think of as color are often referred to as "four color," due to the fact that four different inks are used in them: black, red (magenta), blue (cyan) and yellow. Some magazines also print pages in two color, typically black plus another color.

Front of book (sometimes abbreviated as FOB). The opening pages of a magazine, often home to a table of contents, a masthead, an editor's note, a letters column and assorted small departments.

Galley. The text of a story set in type but not laid out in page form. Many magazines will send you the galleys of your story so you can see how it has been edited and, they hope, catch any errors before it goes to press.

Glossy. A magazine printed on shiny paper rather than the stuff newspapers are made of.

Graf. Shorthand for "paragraph."

Halftone. A photograph after it has been reshot through a screen and converted into a series of tiny dots suitable for printing.

Hed. The headline or title of an article.

House organ. A magazine (or newspaper) published by a company for its employees.

Initial cap. A large capital letter that begins a story or a section of one.

Inventory. See *Bank*.

Jump. Both a verb and a noun: When a magazine article is interrupted on page 34 and continued on page 129, it is said to "jump" to 129, and the part on 129 and later pages is referred to as the "jump."

Kill fee. A partial payment that magazine contracts often promise writers if the magazine decides not to publish an assigned piece. Kill fees often range from 20 percent to 50 percent of the article fee.

Leading. The white space between lines of type. This term goes back to the days when type was still set in the metal lead.

Lede. Jargon for the beginning, or "lead," of a piece.

Line art. A drawing, such as a cartoon.

Little magazine. A magazine with a small circulation, often devoted to literature or politics.

Masthead. The list of people who work on a magazine.

MEGO. One of many mean things that editors sometimes write in the margins of manuscripts (but hopefully not yours). MEGO stands for "My eyes glaze over." In other words, boooooooring.

Multiple submission. A query or a finished piece that a writer has sent to more than one magazine at a time.

News peg. A reason for doing a particular story now instead of last month or next year. A news peg might be something currently in the news or the anniversary of a past news event.

Over the transom. How an unsolicited submission is said to have arrived at the magazine.

Pay on publication (sometimes shorted to "pay on pub"). Most reputable magazines pay a writer when a piece is accepted. But some wait until the piece has actually been published, which can be many months after acceptance. As the American Society of Journalists and Authors wisely points out to its members, "Pay on pub may mean never."

Peg. See *News peg.*

Perfect bound. A squared spine on a magazine.

Phoner. A telephone interview.

Pica. A printer's measurement equal to one-sixth of an inch.

Point. A printer's measurement equal to one-seventy-second of an inch. Type is typically measured in points. For example, the text of a magazine story may be in nine-point type, with the headline in ninety-six-point.

Primary source. For fact-checking purposes, magazines sometimes distinguish between primary and secondary sources. If, for example, you are writing about a television actor, something the actor tells you about himself in the course of an interview would be said to come from a primary source; a quote from the actor copied from another publication is from a secondary source. For obvious reasons, magazines prefer that you go to primary sources when at all possible.

Pull quote. A quotation extracted from your article and repeated in large type to break up an otherwise gray page or to stretch the article enough to fill the page.

Pulp. A magazine printed on cheap, newspaper-like paper. The glory days of the pulps are largely behind us, but a few of them are still kicking.

Q&A. A published interview made up of a series of questions and answers. The famous *Paris Review* interviews reprinted in the *Writers at Work* books are classic examples of the Q&A. Ditto the *Playboy* interview.

Query. A letter from a writer asking an editor whether he or she would be interested in a certain story. See chapter four.

Repositioning. Substantially changing a magazine, often to appeal to a new audience.

SASE. Self-addressed, stamped envelope. Magazines often ask that you enclose one with your queries or other correspondence.

Secondary source. A source that isn't considered primary (see *Primary source*).

Sidebar. A little story that runs with a larger one, often in a box. See chapter thirteen.

Slush pile. Unsolicited manuscripts.

Source list. A list of the people you interviewed and the reference works you consulted. A magazine's fact checkers will use your source list in verifying the information in your article.

Spec. Short for "speculation." Magazines that invite you to submit something "on spec," rather than offering you a contract, will owe you nothing if they decide they don't want to buy your piece.

Spread. Facing pages in a magazine. A "spread opener" means a story that begins on two facing pages, usually to accommodate large artwork.

Stet. An editing instruction, from Latin, meaning "let it stand." You'll often see "stet" written on a galley where something has been changed and the editor thought better of it and went back to the original wording.

Stringer. A freelancer, often one who covers a certain geographic area. Many New York-based magazines, for example, have stringers in Washington, DC or Los Angeles.

Style. A magazine's preferences for the spelling, capitalization, abbreviation or punctuation of certain words or phrases. Some magazines will use the word *catalog*, for example, while others prefer *catalogue*. You can get a sense of a magazine's style by reading it closely.

Tearsheet. A page torn out of a magazine. Writers often use tearsheets as samples of their work. Hint: Rather than literally tear your work out and give the impression that you were in a blind rage at the time, use a sharp knife or razor blade.

TK. An abbreviation meaning "to come." You can use TKs as you write a piece to signal to yourself places where you'll need to come back and fill in a fact. Editors often use TKs to indicate to writers where they want additional facts.

Trade magazine. One people read for business, rather than personal, reasons.

Transparency. A color photograph made with slide film, rather than negative film. Many magazines prefer transparencies to prints because they tend to reproduce more clearly.

Well. A section of pages, sometimes uninterrupted by ads, at the center of many magazines.

Widow. An unsightly, short line at the bottom of a paragraph of type. Magazines that care about such matters will either add more words to the paragraph to lengthen the line or cut enough words to eliminate it. The latter tactic, in rough-and-tumble magazine parlance, is referred to as "killing a widow."

Work made for hire. A rights arrangement in which you sell all the rights in your article to the magazine. See chapter eighteen.

IF NOT NOW, WHEN?

Whether you're a student, a man or woman in the middle of a career, or a retiree, if you've always wanted to write for magazines "someday," that someday is here. There is never a better time than right now to get started.

So go to it—and best of luck. Don't be too discouraged by rejections and don't forget to celebrate your successes. And when in doubt, consult the cover of this book. Remember: "You *Can* Write for Magazines."

INDEX

123